Inglés para camioneros: [8 in 1] Guía práctica de comunicación para transportistas

PUBLISHED BY Carlos M. Salazar

CrossPoint Editions – C. Salazar

© **Copyright 2025 - All rights reserved.**

All introductions, analyses, and commentaries contained within this book may not be reproduced, duplicated, or transmitted without direct written permission from the author or the publisher. Under no circumstances will any blame or legal responsibility be held against the publisher or author for any damages, reparation, or monetary loss due to the information contained within this book, either directly or indirectly.

Legal Notice:

This book is only for personal use. You cannot amend, distribute, sell, use, quote, or paraphrase any part of the introductions, analyses, or commentaries within this book, without the consent of the author or publisher.

Disclaimer Notice:

Please note the information contained within this document is for educational and entertainment purposes only. All efforts have been executed to present accurate, up-to-date, reliable, complete information. No warranties of any kind are declared or implied. Readers acknowledge that the author is not engaged in the rendering of legal, financial, medical, or professional advice. The content within this book has been derived from various sources. Please consult a licensed professional before attempting any techniques outlined in this book.

By reading this document, the reader agrees that under no circumstances is the author responsible for any losses, direct or indirect, that are incurred as a result of the use of the information contained within this document, including, but not limited to, errors, omissions, or inaccuracies.

Table of contents

Introducción 4

Capítulo 1: Comunicación de Emergencia en Carretera 13

Capítulo 2: Comunicación en Cruces Fronterizos y Aduanas 30

Capítulo 3: Inglés para Almacenes y Muelles de Carga . 51

Capítulo 4: Inglés Mecánico y de Mantenimiento 66

Capítulo 5: Comunicación con Despachador y Gestión de Flota 82

Capítulo 6: Servicio al Cliente e Inglés de Entrega 98

Capítulo 7: Cumplimiento Regulatorio y Comunicación DOT 113

Capítulo 8: Servicios de Gasolineras y Paradas de Camiones 130

Introducción

En las primeras horas de una mañana fría de febrero, Miguel Rodríguez se encontró varado en una autopista de Montana con un problema mecánico grave, su carga de productos perecederos perdiendo temperatura rápidamente, y la barrera más frustrante de todas: la incapacidad de explicar su situación de emergencia al mecánico que había llegado para ayudarlo. Después de cuarenta minutos de gestos, dibujos en papel, y la creciente desesperación de ambos hombres, Miguel logró comunicar que necesitaba una reparación urgente del sistema de refrigeración. La reparación que debería haber tomado dos horas se extendió a ocho, resultando en una carga perdida valuada en $15,000, una relación dañada con un cliente importante, y la dolorosa realización de que las habilidades de conducción más expertas del mundo no significan nada si no puedes comunicar tus necesidades profesionales efectivamente.

La historia de Miguel no es única. Representa la experiencia de miles de conductores profesionales hispanohablantes que operan en el mercado de transporte norteamericano, donde la comunicación efectiva en inglés se ha convertido en una habilidad tan esencial como el manejo seguro del vehículo. En una industria donde cada conversación puede afectar la seguridad, la rentabilidad, y las relaciones comerciales que sustentan carreras enteras, las barreras del idioma no son simplemente inconvenientes; son obstáculos significativos que limitan oportunidades, aumentan riesgos, y frecuentemente determinan la diferencia entre el éxito profesional y la lucha constante.

El transporte comercial moderno opera en un ambiente globalizado donde el inglés funciona como el idioma universal del comercio, la logística, y la comunicación regulatoria. Los conductores que dominan la comunicación profesional en inglés acceden a mejores cargas, reciben tratamiento preferencial de despachadores, navegan situaciones de emergencia más efectivamente, y construyen relaciones comerciales que generan oportunidades continuas de crecimiento y prosperidad. Aquellos que luchan con barreras lingüísticas frecuentemente se encuentran limitados a cargas menos deseables, enfrentan malentendidos costosos durante inspecciones regulatorias, y pierden oportunidades de avance que requieren comunicación sofisticada con clientes, supervisores, y autoridades.

La Evolución del Transporte Profesional

La industria del transporte ha experimentado una transformación fundamental en las últimas dos décadas, evolucionando desde operaciones relativamente simples hacia ecosistemas logísticos complejos que integran tecnología avanzada, regulaciones sofisticadas, y expectativas de servicio al cliente que rivalizan con las de cualquier industria de servicios profesionales. Los conductores modernos no son simplemente operadores de vehículos; son profesionales de logística que deben navegar plataformas digitales complejas, comunicarse efectivamente con múltiples stakeholders, y representar sus compañías en interacciones que afectan relaciones comerciales valoradas en millones de dólares.

Este ambiente profesional elevado demanda habilidades de comunicación que van mucho más allá del inglés básico conversacional. Los conductores exitosos deben dominar vocabulario técnico específico para situaciones de emergencia, negociación de rates en plataformas digitales, comunicación regulatoria con oficiales DOT, documentación aduanal para comercio internacional, y servicio al cliente que construye relaciones duraderas que generan negocio repetido y referencias valiosas.

La integración de tecnología en todas las facetas del transporte comercial ha creado oportunidades sin precedentes para conductores que pueden comunicarse efectivamente en inglés a través de múltiples canales digitales. Las plataformas de load matching, sistemas de fleet management, aplicaciones de documentación electrónica, y redes sociales profesionales operan predominantemente en inglés, creando ventajas significativas para drivers que pueden navegar estos sistemas con confianza y competencia profesional.

Simultáneamente, las expectativas regulatorias han aumentado dramáticamente, con inspecciones más rigurosas, documentación más detallada, y comunicación más sofisticada requerida para demostrar cumplimiento con regulaciones federales que afectan todo desde horas de servicio hasta transporte de materiales peligrosos. Los conductores que pueden comunicarse efectivamente durante estas interacciones regulatorias experimentan inspecciones más eficientes, relaciones más positivas con oficiales de enforcement, y significativamente menos probabilidad de violaciones costosas que pueden impactar carreras profesionales.

El Costo de las Barreras Lingüísticas

Las barreras de comunicación en el transporte comercial crean costos que se extienden mucho más allá de la frustración personal, impactando directamente la seguridad pública, la eficiencia económica, y las oportunidades de desarrollo profesional que determinan la trayectoria de carreras enteras.

Los estudios de la industria indican que los malentendidos relacionados con comunicación contribuyen a aproximadamente el 34% de todos los reclamos por daños de carga, resultando en $1.8 mil millones en pérdidas anuales que podrían prevenirse a través de comunicación más efectiva durante procesos de carga, entrega, y documentación. Estas pérdidas no solo afectan a las compañías de transporte y sus clientes, sino que también impactan directamente a los conductores a través de increased insurance premiums, reduced profit sharing, y damaged professional reputations que limitan oportunidades futuras.

Las violaciones regulatorias relacionadas con barreras de comunicación promedian $8,500 en multas y costos asociados por incidente, incluyendo no solo las multas directas sino también tiempo fuera de servicio, costos legales, y impactos en CSA scores que afectan empleabilidad futura y rates de seguro. Más significativamente, estos incidentes frecuentemente resultan de malentendidos durante inspecciones que podrían resolverse fácilmente a través de comunicación clara y profesional.

Los conductores que luchan con barreras de comunicación reportan ingresos anuales que promedian $12,000-$18,000 menos que sus colegas que se comunican efectivamente en inglés, una diferencia que refleja no solo acceso limitado a better-paying loads sino también reduced efficiency en todas las operaciones que afectan earnings potential. Esta brecha de ingresos se amplía con el tiempo a medida que los conductores con strong communication skills acceden a oportunidades de advancement y specialized operations que generan premium compensation.

Una Aproximación Sistemática al Dominio Profesional

Este libro proporciona una aproximación sistemática y comprehensiva para desarrollar las habilidades específicas de comunicación en inglés que determinan el éxito en el transporte comercial moderno. A diferencia de los cursos generales de inglés que se enfocan en conversación casual, este programa está diseñado específicamente para las demandas únicas del transporte profesional, proporcionando vocabulario técnico, estructuras de comunicación, y estrategias interpersonales que se aplican directamente a situaciones reales que los conductores profesionales enfrentan diariamente.

Cada capítulo se enfoca en un área específica de comunicación profesional, proporcionando no solo vocabulario y frases sino también contexto cultural, mejores prácticas, y estrategias para construir relaciones profesionales que sustentan carreras exitosas a largo plazo. Los ejemplos están basados en situaciones reales enfrentadas por conductores profesionales, proporcionando relevancia práctica que permite application inmediata en situaciones de trabajo reales.

El programa reconoce que los conductores profesionales tienen horarios desafiantes y oportunidades limitadas para study tradicional, por lo que está estructurado para permitir learning incremental que puede integrarse con actividades profesionales diarias. Cada interacción profesional se convierte en una oportunidad de práctica, y cada situación exitosa construye confidence para challenges más complejos.

Más Allá del Idioma: Profesionalismo y Oportunidad

El dominio del inglés profesional para conductores comerciales representa mucho más que adquisición de un segundo idioma; constituye una transformation hacia un nivel más elevado de profesionalismo que abre puertas a oportunidades que previamente eran inaccesibles.

Los conductores bilingües que desarrollan strong professional English communication skills frecuentemente acceden a specialized opportunities incluyendo international routes, high-value cargo, customer-facing positions, y leadership roles que ofrecen both higher compensation y greater job satisfaction. Estas oportunidades no están disponibles para conductores monolingües en español o para aquellos cuyas habilidades en inglés están limitadas a comunicación básica.

Las compañías de transporte buscan cada vez más drivers que pueden represent their operations professionally en diverse customer interactions, navigate complex regulatory environments con confidence, y contribute positivamente a la reputation de la company a través de excellent customer service y professional communication. Drivers who develop these capabilities position themselves para preferential treatment en load assignments, equipment assignments, y advancement opportunities.

La industria del transporte continúa evolucionando hacia greater sophistication, technology integration, y customer service excellence que require increasingly advanced communication skills. Drivers who invest en developing these capabilities now position themselves para success en an industry que rewards professionalism y offers substantial opportunities para those prepared para meet elevated expectations.

Tu Inversión en Éxito Profesional

Cada hora que inviertas en desarrollar professional English communication skills representa una inversión en tu future earning potential, career satisfaction, y professional opportunities que se compoundará durante decades de career success. Los beneficios se extienden beyond immediate improvements en daily operations para incluir enhanced reputation, expanded networks, y access para opportunities que pueden transform entire career trajectories.

Professional drivers who master these communication skills reportan not only higher earnings pero también greater job satisfaction, improved relationships con customers y colleagues, y increased confidence en all professional interactions. Esta confidence creates positive cycles donde successful interactions lead para better opportunities, que a su vez provide more practice opportunities y further skill development.

El program presentado en este libro ha sido desarrollado a través de extensive research con successful professional drivers, industry executives, customers, y regulatory officials que han identificado las specific communication skills que distinguish outstanding professionals from average operators. Los strategies y techniques presentados han sido tested y refined through real-world application por hundreds de drivers who han transformed their careers through improved communication capabilities.

Tu journey para master professional English communication comienza con recognition que estas habilidades son not optional luxuries pero essential tools para success en modern commercial transportation. Every conversation, every interaction, y every professional relationship you build contributes para a reputation que opens doors para better opportunities, higher compensation, y greater career satisfaction.

The transportation industry needs professional drivers quien can communicate effectively, represent their companies professionally, y contribute positively para the industry's reputation through excellent customer service y professional competency. By developing these skills, you position yourself not just como a driver, sino como a transportation professional quien adds value para every organization y every customer interaction.

Your commitment para developing these skills demonstrates the same dedication para excellence que characterizes successful careers en any professional field. Como you begin this journey, remember que every expert was once a beginner, y every successful professional communicator developed their skills through practice, persistence, y continuous learning. Your investment en professional English communication skills will pay dividends throughout your career, opening doors para opportunities que will sustain success y satisfaction para years para come.

Capítulo 1: Comunicación de Emergencia en Carretera

En 2023, el 78% de los incidentes de camiones transfronterizos se resolvieron más rápido cuando los conductores pudieron comunicarse efectivamente en inglés con los servicios de emergencia. Esta estadística no es solo un número en un reporte, es la diferencia entre estar varado durante horas o recibir ayuda en minutos. Para miles de conductores profesionales que cruzan fronteras diariamente, el dominio del inglés de emergencia se ha convertido en una herramienta tan esencial como las llaves del camión.

Cuando una situación de emergencia se presenta en la carretera, cada segundo cuenta. La diferencia entre comunicar claramente "I have a blown tire on mile marker 247 southbound" versus intentar explicar la situación con gestos o palabras sueltas puede significar la diferencia entre un servicio de remolque que llega en 30 minutos o uno que tarda dos horas en localizar tu posición exacta.

Este capítulo te equipará con las herramientas lingüísticas fundamentales para enfrentar las situaciones más críticas que cualquier conductor profesional puede experimentar en territorio de habla inglesa. No se trata únicamente de aprender palabras; se trata de desarrollar la confianza y precisión necesarias para actuar como tu propio traductor cuando más lo necesites.

1.1 Reportar Accidentes y Averías

El Arte de la Comunicación Precisa en Momentos Críticos

Imagina esta escena: son las 3:00 AM en una autopista de Montana, la temperatura está bajo cero, y tu camión acaba de experimentar una falla mecánica grave. El dispatcher más cercano está a 200 millas de distancia, y tu teléfono muestra apenas una barra de señal. En este momento, tu capacidad para comunicarte en inglés no es solo conveniente, es literalmente vital.

La comunicación efectiva durante emergencias vehiculares sigue un patrón específico que los servicios de emergencia reconocen inmediatamente. Este patrón incluye tres elementos fundamentales: identificación del problema, ubicación exacta, y nivel de urgencia. Dominar estos elementos en inglés te convertirá en un comunicador más efectivo que muchos conductores nativos del idioma.

Vocabulario Esencial para Describir Daños del Vehículo

El primer paso para una comunicación efectiva es poder describir exactamente qué ha ocurrido con tu vehículo. Los términos técnicos precisos no solo aceleran la respuesta, sino que también ayudan a que llegue el tipo correcto de asistencia.

Inglés para camioneros

Fallas de Llantas y Sistema de Rodamiento:

- "Blown tire" (llanta reventada): Esta es la descripción más precisa cuando una llanta ha perdido presión súbitamente debido a un reventón
- "Flat tire" (llanta desinflada): Se usa cuando la llanta ha perdido presión gradualmente
- "Tire blowout" (reventón de llanta): Describe específicamente el evento cuando la llanta explota mientras conduces
- "Shredded tire" (llanta destrozada): Cuando la llanta se ha desintegrado parcialmente
- "Lost a tire" (perdí una llanta): Cuando la llanta se ha separado completamente del vehículo

Ejemplo de uso: "I have a blown tire on my eighteen-wheeler. The right rear tire on the trailer just blew out."

Problemas del Motor y Sistema Mecánico:

- "Engine failure" (falla del motor): Término general para cualquier problema grave del motor
- "Engine overheating" (sobrecalentamiento del motor): Cuando el motor está operando a temperatura peligrosamente alta
- "Engine seized" (motor gripado): Cuando el motor se ha detenido completamente y no puede girar
- "Transmission failure" (falla de transmisión): Problemas con el sistema de transmisión
- "Brake failure" (falla de frenos): Cuando el sistema de frenos no responde adecuadamente

- "Electrical failure" (falla eléctrica): Problemas con el sistema eléctrico del vehículo
- "Fuel leak" (fuga de combustible): Derrame o goteo de combustible
- "Oil leak" (fuga de aceite): Derrame de aceite del motor
- "Coolant leak" (fuga de refrigerante): Pérdida de líquido refrigerante

Ejemplo de uso: "I'm experiencing engine overheating. The temperature gauge is in the red zone and I can see steam coming from under the hood."

Accidentes y Volcaduras:

- "Rollover" (volcadura): Cuando el vehículo ha girado sobre su costado o techo
- "Jackknife" (deslizamiento lateral en L): Cuando el remolque se dobla en ángulo agudo respecto al tractor
- "Rear-end collision" (colisión por alcance): Choque por detrás
- "Head-on collision" (colisión frontal): Choque de frente
- "Side-swipe" (roce lateral): Contacto lateral entre vehículos
- "Single vehicle accident" (accidente de vehículo único): Accidente que involucra solo tu vehículo
- "Multi-vehicle accident" (accidente de múltiples vehículos): Accidente que involucra varios vehículos

Ejemplo de uso: "I've been involved in a jackknife accident. My trailer has swung around and is blocking two lanes of traffic."

Frases Clave para Descripción de Ubicación

La ubicación precisa es absolutamente crítica en cualquier emergencia. Los servicios de emergencia utilizan sistemas específicos de referencia que debes conocer para comunicar tu posición de manera efectiva.

Usando Marcadores de Millas: Los marcadores de milla son postes verdes con números blancos colocados cada milla a lo largo de las autopistas interestatales. Estos son la forma más precisa de comunicar tu ubicación.

- "I'm at mile marker [número]" (Estoy en el marcador de milla [número])
- "I'm between mile markers [número] and [número]" (Estoy entre los marcadores de milla [número] y [número])
- "I'm approximately half a mile past mile marker [número]" (Estoy aproximadamente media milla después del marcador de milla [número])

Ejemplo: "I'm broken down at mile marker 156 on Interstate 80 eastbound."

Identificando Salidas y Referencias:

- "I'm at exit [número]" (Estoy en la salida [número])
- "I'm [número] miles before exit [número]" (Estoy [número] millas antes de la salida [número])
- "I'm just past the [nombre] exit" (Estoy justo después de la salida de [nombre])

- "I'm at the rest area near exit [número]" (Estoy en el área de descanso cerca de la salida [número])

Direcciones y Carriles:

- "Northbound" (dirección norte)
- "Southbound" (dirección sur)
- "Eastbound" (dirección este)
- "Westbound" (dirección oeste)
- "Right shoulder" (acotamiento derecho)
- "Left shoulder" (acotamiento izquierdo)
- "Center median" (camellón central)
- "Blocking the right lane" (bloqueando el carril derecho)
- "Partially blocking traffic" (bloqueando parcialmente el tráfico)

Coordenadas GPS: Aunque los marcadores de milla son preferidos, las coordenadas GPS son una excelente alternativa:

- "My GPS coordinates are [latitud], [longitud]" (Mis coordenadas GPS son [latitud], [longitud])
- "According to my GPS, I'm at [coordenadas]" (Según mi GPS, estoy en [coordenadas])

Estructuras de Comunicación Urgente

La manera en que estructuras tu llamada de emergencia puede determinar qué tan rápido recibes ayuda. Los operadores de emergencia están entrenados para reconocer ciertos patrones de comunicación que indican diferentes niveles de urgencia.

Inglés para camioneros

Frases de Urgencia Inmediata: Estas frases comunican que necesitas ayuda inmediatamente y que la situación es potencialmente peligrosa:

- "I need immediate assistance" (Necesito asistencia inmediata)
- "This is an emergency" (Esta es una emergencia)
- "I need help right now" (Necesito ayuda ahora mismo)
- "The roadway is blocked" (La carretera está bloqueada)
- "There are injuries involved" (Hay heridos involucrados)
- "I'm in immediate danger" (Estoy en peligro inmediato)

Estructura Recomendada para Llamadas de Emergencia:

1. **Identificación inicial:** "This is a truck driver with an emergency"
2. **Ubicación inmediata:** "I'm at mile marker [número] on [autopista] [dirección]"
3. **Naturaleza del problema:** "I have a [descripción del problema]"
4. **Nivel de urgencia:** "I need immediate assistance" o "This is not immediately dangerous, but I need help"
5. **Información adicional:** Detalles sobre heridos, bloqueo de tráfico, materiales peligrosos, etc.

Ejemplo de llamada completa: "This is a truck driver with an emergency. I'm at mile marker 89 on Interstate 75 northbound. I've been involved in a jackknife accident. The roadway is partially blocked, but there are no injuries. I need immediate assistance to clear the road and get my vehicle moved."

Para Situaciones Menos Urgentes:

- "I'm broken down and need a tow truck" (Estoy varado y necesito una grúa)
- "I have a mechanical problem" (Tengo un problema mecánico)
- "I need roadside assistance" (Necesito asistencia en carretera)
- "This is not an emergency, but I need help" (Esto no es una emergencia, pero necesito ayuda)

Información Adicional Importante: Siempre mantén lista la siguiente información para proporcionar cuando te la soliciten:

- Número de placas del vehículo
- Compañía para la que trabajas
- Tipo de carga que transportas
- Tu número de licencia de conducir
- Información del seguro

Comunicando Sobre Materiales Peligrosos: Si transportas materiales peligrosos, esto debe comunicarse inmediatamente:

- "I'm hauling hazardous materials" (Estoy transportando materiales peligrosos)
- "I have a placard number [número]" (Tengo el número de placa [número])
- "There is no leak or spill" (No hay fuga o derrame)
- "There is a possible leak" (Hay una posible fuga)

La comunicación efectiva durante emergencias no es solo sobre conocer las palabras correctas; es sobre mantener la calma, ser preciso, y proporcionar exactamente la información que los servicios de emergencia necesitan para ayudarte de la manera más rápida y segura posible. Cada palabra que elijas puede hacer la diferencia entre una resolución rápida y una situación que se prolonga innecesariamente.

1.2 Comunicación con Servicios de Emergencia

La diferencia entre un operador 911, un despachador de patrulla de carreteras y un representante de asistencia en carretera puede parecer insignificante cuando estás enfrentando una emergencia, pero entender estas distinciones puede acelerar dramáticamente el tiempo de respuesta y asegurar que recibas exactamente el tipo de ayuda que necesitas.

Navegando los Diferentes Protocolos de Emergencia

Cada sistema de emergencia opera bajo protocolos específicos diseñados para maximizar la eficiencia y la seguridad. El sistema 911 es tu primer recurso para emergencias que involucran lesiones, materiales peligrosos derramados, o situaciones que representen peligro inmediato para ti o para otros conductores. Cuando llamas al 911, el operador seguirá un protocolo estricto que incluye verificar tu ubicación, evaluar la naturaleza de la emergencia, y determinar qué tipo de respuesta se necesita.

Los operadores 911 están entrenados para hacer preguntas específicas en una secuencia particular. Esperarán que respondas de manera directa y concisa. Frases como "I need police, fire, or ambulance" te conectarán inmediatamente con el departamento apropiado. Es crucial entender que interrumpir al operador o proporcionar información fuera de secuencia puede retrasar la respuesta.

La patrulla de carreteras, por otro lado, se enfoca específicamente en incidentes relacionados con el tráfico y la seguridad vial. Cuando contactas directamente a la patrulla de carreteras, sus despachadores están preparados para manejar situaciones como vehículos varados, accidentes menores sin lesiones, y problemas de tráfico. Su protocolo incluye preguntas detalladas sobre la posición de tu vehículo en relación con el flujo de tráfico, si represents un peligro para otros conductores, y si necesitas que controlen el tráfico mientras esperas asistencia.

Los servicios de asistencia en carretera comerciales operan bajo un modelo completamente diferente. Sus representantes están enfocados en la logística de proporcionar servicio mecánico, remolque, o reparaciones menores. Sus preguntas se centrarán en el tipo específico de vehículo que conduces, la naturaleza exacta del problema mecánico, y si tienes cobertura de servicio a través de tu empleador o una póliza personal.

Comunicación de Emergencias Médicas

Las situaciones médicas en carretera requieren un vocabulario específico que los paramédicos y personal de emergencias médicas reconocen inmediatamente. La precisión en tu descripción puede influenciar qué tipo de equipo médico se envía a tu ubicación y qué tan rápido llegan.

Para lesiones personales, necesitas comunicar tres elementos críticos: el tipo de lesión, la gravedad aparente, y el estado de conciencia de la persona lesionada. Si te has lastimado, frases como "I think I have a broken arm" o "I'm experiencing chest pain" proporcionan información médica inicial crucial. Para lesiones más graves, "I'm having trouble breathing" o "I think I'm having a heart attack" activarán protocolos de respuesta de alta prioridad.

Cuando describes lesiones de otros, la objetividad es esencial. "The other driver appears to be unconscious" es más útil que "I think he might be sleeping." Si hay sangrado visible, describe la ubicación y la cantidad aparente: "There's heavy bleeding from his head" o "She has what appears to be a broken leg with some bleeding."

El estado de conciencia es particularmente importante para el personal médico. Términos como "conscious and alert," "conscious but confused," "unconscious but breathing," o "unconscious and not breathing" proporcionan información vital que determina el nivel de respuesta médica necesaria.

Para situaciones que involucran múltiples víctimas, necesitas proporcionar un conteo inicial: "There are three people injured, two appear conscious, one is unconscious." Esta información ayuda a los despachadores a determinar cuántas ambulancias enviar y si necesitan activar protocolos de incidente de múltiples víctimas.

Manejo de Preguntas sobre Cargas Peligrosas

Los despachadores de emergencia están específicamente entrenados para hacer preguntas detalladas sobre materiales peligrosos porque esta información determina qué tipo de personal especializado necesitan enviar y qué precauciones de seguridad deben tomar.

Cuando transportas materiales peligrosos, el número de placa en tu vehículo es la información más importante que puedes proporcionar. Este número de cuatro dígitos le dice inmediatamente al despachador exactamente qué tipo de material estás transportando y cuáles son los riesgos asociados. "I'm hauling hazmat, placard number 1203" proporciona información instantánea sobre gasolina, mientras que "placard number 1005" indica amoníaco anhidro.

Si no puedes ver claramente el número de placa debido a daño del vehículo o condiciones de visibilidad, proporciona toda la información que puedas: "I'm hauling fuel, but I can't see the placard number clearly." Los despachadores prefieren información parcial a adivinanzas incorrectas.

La condición del contenedor es igualmente importante. "The tank appears intact" versus "I can see liquid leaking from the tank" representa la diferencia entre un incidente de rutina y una emergencia de materiales peligrosos que requiere evacuación del área. Si detectas cualquier olor inusual, esto debe comunicarse inmediatamente: "I smell a strong chemical odor" puede indicar una fuga peligrosa incluso si no puedes ver daño visible.

Para cargas no peligrosas, aún necesitas proporcionar información básica sobre qué estás transportando. "I'm hauling general freight" o "I have a load of automotive parts" ayuda a los servicios de emergencia a entender si hay algún riesgo secundario o consideraciones especiales para mover tu vehículo.

1.3 Comunicación de Seguros y Legal

La documentación precisa de incidentes en inglés no es simplemente una formalidad burocrática; es tu protección legal y financiera más importante cuando operas en territorio de habla inglesa. La manera en que describes un incidente puede determinar si tu reclamo de seguro es aprobado o denegado, y si enfrentas responsabilidad legal o quedas exonerado.

Documentación de Incidentes para Seguros y Reportes Policiales

Cuando documentes un incidente para propósitos de seguros, la objetividad y la precisión son fundamentales. Los ajustadores de seguros están entrenados para identificar inconsistencias en los reportes, y cualquier descripción que parezca subjetiva o emocional puede ser utilizada para cuestionar tu credibilidad.

La secuencia de eventos debe describirse en tiempo pasado y en orden cronológico. "I was traveling eastbound on Interstate 40 at approximately 65 mph when the vehicle in front of me stopped suddenly" establece claramente las circunstancias iniciales. Evita frases como "the idiot in front of me slammed on his brakes" porque introducen opiniones personales que no ayudan a establecer los hechos.

Las condiciones del clima y la carretera son factores críticos que deben documentarse precisamente. "The roadway was wet from recent rain" es más útil que "it was kind of slippery." La visibilidad también debe describirse objetivamente: "Visibility was reduced due to fog" o "The sun was directly in my line of sight" son descripciones que los ajustadores pueden evaluar objetivamente.

Cuando describas daños al vehículo, usa terminología específica. "The front bumper has a dent approximately two feet wide" es más preciso que "the front end is messed up." Para daños internos, "The engine is making unusual noises and losing power" describe síntomas observables que los mecánicos pueden evaluar.

Las declaraciones de testigos deben registrarse exactamente como fueron hechas, usando comillas para indicar palabras textuales. "The witness stated, 'I saw the truck try to stop but couldn't avoid the collision'" proporciona evidencia de terceros que puede ser crucial para tu caso.

Comprensión de Derechos Durante Paradas de Tráfico e Inspecciones DOT

Entender tus derechos durante paradas de tráfico e inspecciones del Departamento de Transporte no se trata de ser confrontativo; se trata de proteger tus intereses legales mientras mantienes una relación profesional con las autoridades.

Durante una parada de tráfico rutinaria, tienes el derecho de permanecer callado más allá de proporcionar tu licencia, registro del vehículo, y prueba de seguro. Sin embargo, la comunicación cooperativa generalmente resulta en una interacción más rápida y menos problemática. "Good morning, officer. Here's my license and registration" establece un tono profesional y cooperativo.

Si un oficial solicita registrar tu vehículo sin una orden de cateo, tienes el derecho de preguntar "Do you have a warrant to search my vehicle?" Esta no es una pregunta confrontativa; es una consulta legítima sobre tus derechos constitucionales. Si el oficial indica que tiene causa probable, puedes declarar "I do not consent to this search, but I will not resist" para proteger tus derechos legales mientras evitas escalación física.

Las inspecciones DOT operan bajo reglas diferentes porque los vehículos comerciales están sujetos a regulaciones federales específicas. Durante una inspección DOT, los oficiales tienen autoridad amplia para examinar tu vehículo, documentos, y registros de horas de servicio. Tu cooperación durante estas inspecciones es requerida por ley, pero aún tienes derecho a entender qué están buscando específicamente.

Cuando un inspector DOT encuentra una violación, tienes el derecho de recibir una explicación clara de la infracción. "Can you explain exactly what regulation I've violated?" es una pregunta apropiada que puede ayudarte a entender cómo evitar problemas similares en el futuro. Si no estás de acuerdo con una citación, puedes declarar "I respectfully disagree with this citation and intend to contest it" sin admitir culpabilidad.

Rechazando Cargas Inseguras y Reportando Violaciones

La presión económica para aceptar cargas problemáticas es una realidad en la industria del transporte, pero existen maneras profesionales de rechazar asignaciones inseguras sin poner en riesgo tu empleo.

Cuando una carga parece insegura, documenta tus preocupaciones específicas antes de comunicarte con tu despachador. "The load appears to exceed weight limits for this trailer" es una observación objetiva basada en regulaciones federales. "I'm concerned about the securement of this load based on DOT regulations" indica que tu rechazo está basado en cumplimiento regulatorio, no en preferencia personal.

La comunicación con tu empleador sobre cargas inseguras debe enfocarse en la protección tanto tuya como de la compañía. "I'm concerned that accepting this load could result in DOT violations that would affect both my CDL and the company's safety rating" enmarca tu preocupación en términos de riesgo empresarial compartido.

Para reportar violaciones de seguridad, necesitas distinguir entre problemas internos de la compañía y violaciones que requieren reporte a autoridades externas. Problemas como presión para violar regulaciones de horas de servicio pueden inicialmente dirigirse a supervisores con "I need to report that I'm being asked to drive beyond legal hour limits." Si la presión continúa después de esta comunicación interna, entonces el reporte a autoridades federales puede ser necesario.

Cuando reportes violaciones a agencias externas como FMCSA, la documentación debe ser específica y verificable. "On [fecha], I was instructed by [nombre/título] to drive beyond my available hours" proporciona información específica que las agencias pueden investigar. "I have documentation showing [tipo de evidencia]" indica que tienes evidencia de respaldo para tus afirmaciones.

La protección contra represalias por reportar violaciones de seguridad está garantizada por ley federal, pero ejercer esta protección requiere documentación cuidadosa. "I am filing this complaint under whistleblower protections" establece claramente que entiendes tus derechos legales. Mantén copias de toda comunicación relacionada con reportes de seguridad, incluyendo fechas, nombres de personas involucradas, y descripciones específicas de las violaciones reportadas.

La comunicación efectiva en situaciones legales y de seguros no se trata de evitar responsabilidad cuando eres culpable; se trata de asegurar que los hechos se presenten claramente y que tus derechos sean respetados durante todo el proceso. La precisión en el lenguaje y la comprensión de tus derechos te protegen tanto legal como profesionalmente.

Capítulo 2: Comunicación en Cruces Fronterizos y Aduanas

Una sola mala comunicación en la frontera puede costarle a los camioneros un promedio de 4-6 horas en retrasos y hasta $2,000 en multas. Esta realidad se vuelve aún más costosa cuando consideramos el tiempo perdido, la carga que se deteriora, y los clientes insatisfechos que pueden cancelar contratos futuros. Para los conductores que cruzan regularmente entre México, Estados Unidos y Canadá, dominar la comunicación aduanal en inglés no es solo una ventaja competitiva, es una necesidad económica fundamental.

Los cruces fronterizos operan en un mundo donde la precisión del lenguaje puede significar la diferencia entre un cruce de rutina de 30 minutos y una pesadilla burocrática de varios días. Cada documento, cada clasificación de carga, y cada respuesta que das a los oficiales aduanales puede desencadenar inspecciones adicionales o facilitar un tránsito sin problemas.

Este capítulo te dará las herramientas lingüísticas específicas para navegar el complejo mundo de la documentación aduanal, explicar discrepancias cuando surjan, y comunicarte con autoridad y precisión sobre tu carga, independientemente de qué tan complicada sea la situación.

2.1 Discusiones sobre Documentación y Papeleo

La Complejidad Oculta de la Documentación Aduanal

Los cruces fronterizos comerciales operan bajo un sistema documental que puede parecer redundante para quienes no están familiarizados con él, pero cada documento cumple una función específica en la cadena de custodia y cumplimiento regulatorio. El conocimiento de embarque, el manifiesto de carga, y los permisos especiales forman un ecosistema documental donde la inconsistencia en cualquier elemento puede desencadenar investigaciones exhaustivas.

El conocimiento de embarque, conocido en inglés como "bill of lading" o simplemente "BOL," es efectivamente el certificado de nacimiento de tu carga. Este documento establece qué mercancía está siendo transportada, quién es el remitente, quién es el destinatario, y bajo qué términos se está realizando el transporte. Cuando un oficial aduanal encuentra una discrepancia en el BOL, no está simplemente verificando papeleo; está investigando una posible violación de múltiples regulaciones federales.

El manifiesto de carga, referido como "cargo manifest" en inglés, proporciona una vista consolidada de todo lo que está cruzando la frontera en tu vehículo. Mientras que el BOL describe la relación comercial, el manifiesto describe la realidad física de lo que estás transportando. Esta distinción es crucial porque los oficiales aduanales están entrenados para identificar discrepancias entre lo que los documentos declaran y lo que realmente está en tu trailer.

Los permisos especiales, que pueden incluir desde "oversize load permits" hasta "hazmat transportation permits," representan autorizaciones gubernamentales específicas para transportar cargas que de otro modo serían ilegales o restringidas. Estos permisos a menudo tienen condiciones específicas de tiempo, ruta, y equipamiento que deben cumplirse exactamente como están escritas.

Navegando Discrepancias en el Conocimiento de Embarque

Cuando los oficiales aduanales identifican discrepancias en tu documentación, tu respuesta inicial determina si la situación se resuelve rápidamente o se convierte en una investigación prolongada. La clave está en demostrar que entiendes la naturaleza de la discrepancia y que tienes una explicación legítima respaldada por documentación adicional.

Si un oficial señala una discrepancia en el peso declarado versus el peso real de tu carga, una respuesta efectiva podría ser: "I understand there's a weight discrepancy. The bill of lading shows [peso declarado], but the actual weight at the scale is [peso real]. I have the certified scale ticket from the shipper that shows the discrepancy occurred at loading." Esta respuesta demuestra que reconoces el problema, proporcionas los datos específicos, y tienes documentación de respaldo.

Para discrepancias en la descripción de la mercancía, la precisión técnica es esencial. Si tu BOL declara "automotive parts" pero la inspección revela componentes específicos que podrían estar sujetos a regulaciones diferentes, necesitas poder explicar: "The bill of lading uses the general term 'automotive parts,' but specifically I'm carrying brake pads, alternators, and air filters. I have the detailed packing list that breaks down each component if you need to see it."

Las discrepancias en las direcciones de origen o destino requieren un enfoque particularmente cuidadoso porque pueden indicar intentos de evadir ciertos aranceles o regulaciones. Una explicación apropiada podría ser: "The shipper's address on the BOL shows their corporate headquarters, but the actual pickup was at their warehouse facility. I have the pickup receipt with the warehouse address and can provide the shipper's contact information to verify this arrangement."

Cuando las fechas en los documentos no coinciden, esto puede señalar problemas de cumplimiento de tiempo de tránsito o intentos de manipular cronogramas para propósitos arancelarios. Una respuesta clara sería: "The original shipping date was delayed due to [razón específica]. I have documentation from the shipper explaining the delay and authorizing the revised timeline."

Clasificaciones de Carga y Sus Implicaciones Regulatorias

El sistema de clasificación de carga internacional opera bajo códigos específicos que determinan todo, desde aranceles hasta restricciones de importación. Entender estos sistemas y poder comunicarte sobre ellos en inglés es crucial para explicar tu carga cuando surgen preguntas.

El Sistema Armonizado, conocido como "Harmonized System" o "HS codes," proporciona códigos numéricos de seis dígitos para prácticamente todas las mercancías comerciables. Cuando un oficial aduanal pregunta sobre la clasificación de tu carga, necesitas poder responder con precisión: "The HS code for this merchandise is 8708.30, which covers brake pads and other brake system components for motor vehicles."

Las clasificaciones NAFTA, ahora bajo el USMCA (United States-Mexico-Canada Agreement), tienen sus propias complejidades. Poder explicar: "This cargo qualifies for preferential NAFTA treatment under classification [código] because it meets the regional value content requirements" demuestra comprensión sofisticada de comercio internacional.

Para materiales peligrosos, las clasificaciones DOT y UN son fundamentales. "This shipment is classified as UN 1203, which is gasoline, and it's properly placarded and documented according to DOT hazmat regulations" proporciona la información específica que los oficiales necesitan para evaluar el cumplimiento.

Las restricciones estacionales afectan ciertos productos agrícolas y alimentarios. Poder explicar: "I understand this produce is subject to seasonal import restrictions. I have the USDA import permit and the phytosanitary certificate showing compliance with current regulations" demuestra preparación profesional.

Las clasificaciones de textiles bajo el sistema de cuotas textiles requieren documentación específica. Una explicación apropiada sería: "These garments are classified under textile category [número] and I have the required export visa from the country of origin showing quota availability."

Solicitando Aclaración sobre Formularios y Regulaciones

La capacidad de solicitar aclaración de manera profesional cuando no entiendes algo es tan importante como proporcionar respuestas correctas. Los oficiales aduanales aprecian la honestidad sobre la confusión más que las adivinanzas incorrectas que pueden complicar la situación.

Cuando encuentres un formulario que no has visto antes, una aproximación efectiva es: "I'm not familiar with this particular form. Could you explain what information you need and how it relates to my shipment?" Esta pregunta demuestra que quieres cumplir pero necesitas orientación específica.

Para regulaciones que han cambiado recientemente, puedes preguntar: "I want to make sure I understand the current requirements. Has there been a recent change to the regulations for this type of cargo?" Esta pregunta muestra conciencia de que las regulaciones evolucionan y que quieres mantenerte actualizado.

Si te piden documentación que crees que no se aplica a tu carga, una respuesta apropiada sería: "I want to make sure I understand correctly. You're asking for [tipo de documento] for [tipo de carga]. Could you help me understand why this document is required for this particular shipment?"

Cuando las instrucciones sobre formularios no están claras, es mejor preguntar: "I want to complete this form correctly. For section [número], when it asks for [información específica], are you looking for [tu interpretación] or something else?"

Para situaciones donde múltiples regulaciones parecen aplicar, puedes decir: "I see that this cargo might fall under several different regulatory categories. Could you help me determine which specific requirements apply in this case?"

Manejando Formularios Aduanales Complejos

Los formularios aduanales modernos están diseñados para capturar información específica que alimenta sistemas de análisis de riesgo automatizados. Entender la lógica detrás de las preguntas te ayuda a proporcionar respuestas que faciliten el procesamiento eficiente.

El Formulario 7501 de CBP (U.S. Customs and Border Protection Entry Summary) requiere información detallada sobre el valor, clasificación, y origen de la mercancía. Cuando los oficiales cuestionan entradas específicas en este formulario, necesitas poder explicar: "The declared value of [cantidad] represents the transaction value as required by CBP regulations. I have the commercial invoice supporting this valuation."

Para el Formulario CF 3461 (Entry/Immediate Delivery), que permite liberación inmediata de ciertas mercancías, puedes necesitar explicar: "This shipment qualifies for immediate delivery processing because it consists of [tipo de mercancía] from a trusted trader with established compliance history."

Los manifiestos de camión requieren información específica sobre el vehículo, conductor, y carga. Si hay discrepancias, una explicación podría ser: "The manifest shows my previous trailer number because we switched trailers at the pickup point due to mechanical issues. I have the equipment interchange receipt documenting the change."

Para cargas que requieren inspección previa, como ciertos productos agrícolas, necesitas poder explicar: "This produce has been pre-inspected at the facility of origin. I have the USDA inspection certificate and the sealed container documentation showing the chain of custody has been maintained."

Cuando transportas mercancía en tránsito que no está destinada al país por el que estás pasando, la documentación de tránsito es crucial: "This is an in-transit shipment from [país de origen] to [país de destino]. I have the TIR carnet and all required transit documentation showing this cargo will not enter commerce in this country."

Comunicación Sobre Valores y Aranceles

Las discusiones sobre valoración aduanal requieren precisión técnica porque afectan directamente los aranceles que se deben pagar. Cuando los oficiales cuestionan el valor declarado de tu carga, necesitas entender la diferencia entre varios métodos de valoración.

El método de valor de transacción, que es el más común, se basa en el precio realmente pagado: "The declared value represents the actual transaction value between the buyer and seller, as shown on the commercial invoice. This includes the cost of the goods plus shipping to the point of exportation."

Para situaciones donde el valor de transacción no puede determinarse, puedes necesitar explicar métodos alternativos: "Since this is a related-party transaction, the value has been determined using the deductive value method based on comparable sales in the domestic market."

Cuando hay ajustes al valor por servicios adicionales, la explicación podría ser: "The declared value includes assists provided by the buyer, specifically engineering services valued at [cantidad], as required by CBP valuation regulations."

Para mercancía usada o remanufacturada, la valoración puede ser compleja: "This equipment is classified as used machinery. The declared value reflects the fair market value of comparable used equipment, supported by an independent appraisal."

Las situaciones de garantía temporal requieren explicaciones específicas: "This machinery is being temporarily imported for demonstration purposes under a temporary importation bond. It will be re-exported within [período de tiempo] and no duties are due at this time."

La comunicación efectiva en cruces fronterizos no se trata solo de tener la documentación correcta; se trata de poder explicar esa documentación de manera clara, responder preguntas con confianza, y demostrar que entiendes tanto las regulaciones como el negocio que estás representando. Cada interacción con oficiales aduanales es una oportunidad de construir tu reputación como un conductor profesional que facilita el comercio internacional de manera legal y eficiente.

2.2 Procedimientos de Inspección y Cumplimiento

Los procedimientos de inspección en cruces fronterizos han evolucionado dramáticamente en la última década, transformándose de verificaciones básicas de documentos a sistemas sofisticados que integran tecnología de escaneo, análisis de datos biométricos, y evaluación de riesgo en tiempo real. Para los conductores profesionales, entender no solo qué pueden solicitar los inspectores, sino cómo comunicarse efectivamente durante estos procedimientos, puede ser la diferencia entre una inspección de rutina de 45 minutos y una revisión exhaustiva de varias horas.

Navegando Comandos y Solicitudes de Inspección

Los inspectores aduanales y de DOT están entrenados para dar comandos específicos que deben seguirse exactamente como se indican. La cooperación inmediata y clara no solo acelera el proceso, sino que también establece un tono profesional que puede influenciar positivamente toda la interacción.

Cuando un inspector dice "Pull forward to bay number three," la respuesta apropiada es "Yes sir, pulling forward to bay three now." Esta confirmación verbal demuestra que has entendido la instrucción y estás cumpliendo inmediatamente. Evita respuestas como "okay" o simplemente asentir con la cabeza, ya que los inspectores necesitan confirmación verbal clara para sus registros.

Para solicitudes de documentación, como "I need to see your logbook, bill of lading, and driver's license," la mejor práctica es confirmar cada documento mientras lo entregas: "Here's my driver's license, this is the current logbook, and here's the bill of lading for this shipment." Esta práctica ayuda a prevenir confusiones sobre qué documentos has proporcionado y cuáles aún pueden necesitarse.

Cuando los inspectores solicitan acceso físico a tu carga con frases como "I need you to open the trailer doors," tu respuesta debe incluir cualquier información relevante sobre la seguridad de la carga: "I'll open the doors now. Please note that this is a sealed load and I have the seal numbers documented here." Si hay consideraciones especiales, como carga refrigerada, debes mencionarlo inmediatamente: "I'm opening the doors now, but this is a temperature-controlled load, so I'll need to close them as soon as possible to maintain the cold chain."

Las solicitudes para inspección de equipamiento requieren respuestas que demuestren tu conocimiento profesional. Cuando un inspector dice "Show me your pre-trip inspection report," puedes responder: "Here's today's pre-trip inspection. I completed it this morning before departure and documented these minor issues that don't affect safety or operation."

Explicando Números de Sello y Registros de Cadena de Custodia

Los números de sello son elementos críticos en la cadena de custodia internacional, y los inspectores están específicamente entrenados para verificar que estos números coincidan exactamente con la documentación. Cualquier discrepancia puede indicar posible manipulación de la carga o problemas de seguridad.

Cuando presentes números de sello, la precisión es fundamental: "The seal number on the trailer is [número exacto], which matches the seal number documented on the bill of lading and the customs manifest." Si hay múltiples sellos, como en cargas de alto valor, debes explicar cada uno: "There are two seals on this trailer. The primary customs seal is [número], and there's also a shipper's security seal numbered [número] applied at the facility of origin."

Para situaciones donde los sellos han sido cambiados durante el tránsito, la documentación debe ser exhaustiva: "The original seal [número original] was removed by customs authorities at [ubicación] for inspection. The new seal [número nuevo] was applied by the same authorities, and I have the official documentation of the seal change here."

Los registros de temperatura para cargas refrigeradas requieren explicaciones técnicas específicas. "The temperature log shows consistent readings between [rango de temperatura] throughout the journey. The refrigeration unit is set to maintain [temperatura específica] as required by the shipper, and I have hourly temperature recordings for the entire trip."

Cuando los inspectores cuestionan variaciones de temperatura, tu explicación debe ser técnica y precisa: "There was a brief temperature spike to [temperatura] during the fuel stop at [ubicación], but it returned to the required range within fifteen minutes. This is within acceptable parameters for this type of product, and I have documentation from the shipper confirming these tolerance levels."

Especificaciones de Equipamiento y Cumplimiento Técnico

Los inspectores de DOT están particularmente enfocados en el cumplimiento técnico del equipamiento, y tu capacidad para explicar las especificaciones de tu equipo demuestra profesionalismo y conocimiento de las regulaciones.

Para inspecciones de frenos, necesitas poder explicar el sistema de tu vehículo: "This truck is equipped with an air brake system with automatic slack adjusters. The brake chambers are all within specification, and I performed a brake inspection this morning showing [mediciones específicas] on the push rod travel."

Las inspecciones de llantas requieren conocimiento técnico específico: "All tires are rated for the current load weight. The steer tires are [especificación], the drive tires are [especificación], and the trailer tires are [especificación]. I have documentation showing the last tire inspection was performed [fecha] with all tires meeting DOT standards."

Para equipamiento de materiales peligrosos, las explicaciones deben ser exhaustivas: "This vehicle is properly equipped for hazmat transportation with [lista de equipamiento]. The fire extinguisher was last inspected [fecha], the spill kit is complete and current, and all placards are properly displayed according to the cargo being transported."

Comunicación sobre Horas de Servicio y Registros ELD

Los dispositivos de registro electrónico han revolucionado la manera en que se monitorean las horas de servicio, pero también han creado nuevas complejidades en la comunicación con inspectores que necesitan entender tu estatus de cumplimiento.

Cuando un inspector solicita revisar tu ELD, la presentación debe ser organizada: "Here's my ELD display showing current hours. I'm currently on line [número de línea de servicio] with [tiempo restante] remaining on my drive time. My last required rest period was completed [tiempo y ubicación], and my next mandatory break is due at [tiempo]."

Para explicar violaciones de HOS que puedan aparecer en tu registro, la honestidad combinada con explicaciones específicas es crucial: "The ELD shows a form and manner violation from [fecha]. This occurred when I was delayed at a shipper for [razón específica] beyond my control. I have documentation from the shipper confirming the delay and showing that I took all required rest as soon as I was released."

Las situaciones de mal funcionamiento del ELD requieren explicaciones técnicas: "My ELD experienced a malfunction starting [fecha y hora]. I immediately switched to paper logs as required by regulation and have documentation of the malfunction. The device has been repaired and is now functioning normally, with all data properly recorded."

Registros del Conductor y Documentación Personal

Los inspectores revisan registros del conductor no solo para verificar cumplimiento de HOS, sino también para evaluar patrones de comportamiento y profesionalismo general.

Tu Medical Examiner's Certificate debe presentarse con confianza: "Here's my current DOT physical card. It's valid until [fecha de vencimiento], and I don't have any restrictions or limitations on my certification."

Para tu Commercial Driver's License, la presentación debe incluir información relevante: "This is my current CDL with [endorsements específicos]. It's valid in all states and I don't have any pending violations or restrictions."

Los registros de Vehicle Inspection Reports deben estar organizados y actualizados: "Here are my daily inspection reports for the past [período]. All defects identified have been properly repaired, and I have documentation showing the repairs were completed by qualified personnel."

2.3 Resolución de Problemas en Fronteras

Las situaciones problemáticas en cruces fronterizos requieren un delicado equilibrio entre firmeza profesional y cooperación diplomática. Los conductores experimentados entienden que la manera en que manejas los primeros minutos de un problema puede determinar si se resuelve rápidamente o se convierte en una crisis que consume días y miles de dólares.

Negociando Tiempos de Espera y Comunicando Urgencia

Las cargas sensibles al tiempo presentan desafíos únicos en cruces fronterizos donde los retrasos pueden resultar en pérdidas financieras significativas. La clave está en comunicar urgencia sin parecer agresivo o irrespetuoso hacia los procedimientos oficiales.

Cuando transportes productos perecederos, tu comunicación inicial debe establecer inmediatamente la naturaleza sensible al tiempo de tu carga: "I want to inform you that I'm carrying perishable produce that's temperature-sensitive and time-critical. The load needs to reach its destination by [tiempo específico] to maintain quality standards and meet contractual obligations."

Para cargas médicas o farmacéuticas, la urgencia puede ser aún más crítica: "This shipment contains medical supplies that are needed for patient care. I have documentation showing the critical timeline for delivery, and any significant delay could impact patient treatment schedules."

La manufactura just-in-time crea sus propias presiones de tiempo: "I'm carrying automotive parts for a just-in-time manufacturing line that's scheduled to begin production at [tiempo específico]. A delay beyond [tiempo límite] would shut down the production line and affect hundreds of workers."

Cuando solicites expedición del procesamiento, siempre proporciona soluciones específicas: "Given the time-sensitive nature of this cargo, would it be possible to expedite the inspection process? I have all documentation ready, and I'm prepared to assist in any way that might speed up the procedure while maintaining all security requirements."

Abordando Errores de Documentación Sin Admitir Culpa

Los errores de documentación son inevitables en el comercio internacional complejo, pero la manera en que los abordas puede determinar si resultan en multas menores o problemas legales serios.

Cuando identifiques un error en tus documentos, la comunicación inmediata es crucial: "I've noticed there appears to be an error in [documento específico]. The [campo específico] shows [información incorrecta], but it should show [información correcta]. I want to address this immediately to avoid any compliance issues."

Para errores que no fueron causados por ti, la explicación debe ser factual sin asignar culpa: "There appears to be a discrepancy between the shipper's documentation and what's shown on the customs paperwork. I have the original documents from the shipper that show [información correcta], and I believe this may be a clerical error that occurred during document preparation."

Cuando los errores podrían afectar aranceles o clasificaciones, tu comunicación debe ser especialmente cuidadosa: "I want to ensure complete accuracy in the documentation. I believe there may be an error in the classification code that could affect the duty calculation. I have additional documentation that might help clarify the correct classification."

Para situaciones donde múltiples partes están involucradas en la preparación de documentos: "The documentation was prepared by [parte responsable], and I want to verify that all information is accurate. If there are any discrepancies, I have contact information for the responsible party who can provide corrections or clarifications."

Escalación Profesional y Solicitud de Supervisión

Saber cuándo y cómo solicitar supervisión adicional es una habilidad crítica que puede resolver problemas que de otro modo se prolongarían indefinidamente.

Cuando sientas que un inspector no está manejando tu situación apropiadamente, la escalación debe ser respetuosa pero firme: "I appreciate your assistance with this matter, but I believe there may be some confusion about the regulations that apply to this shipment. Would it be possible to speak with a supervisor who might have additional expertise in this area?"

Para situaciones donde sientes que estás siendo tratado injustamente: "I want to ensure that I'm receiving fair treatment under the regulations. Could I please speak with a supervisor to review the procedures being applied to my shipment?"

Cuando las regulaciones parecen estar siendo aplicadas incorrectamente: "I believe there may be a misunderstanding about which regulations apply to this situation. I'd like to request a supervisor's review to ensure we're following the correct procedures."

Solicitud de Servicios de Traducción

Aunque tu objetivo es comunicarte efectivamente en inglés, hay situaciones donde la precisión técnica o legal requiere servicios de traducción profesional.

Para documentos complejos en español que necesitan traducción: "I have supporting documentation in Spanish that I believe is relevant to this inspection. Would it be possible to have these documents translated to ensure complete understanding?"

Cuando cuestiones técnicas complejas están involucradas: "Given the technical complexity of this issue and the potential legal implications, I would like to request interpreter services to ensure complete accuracy in our communication."

Para situaciones donde malentendidos han complicado el proceso: "I'm concerned that there may have been miscommunication that's complicating this process. Could we have an interpreter present to ensure complete clarity in our discussion?"

Gestión de Crisis y Comunicación de Contingencia

Cuando los problemas fronterizos se vuelven serios, tu comunicación debe volverse más formal y documentada.

Para retrasos que afectarán compromisos contractuales: "Due to the extended inspection process, I need to notify my dispatcher and customer about potential delivery delays. Could you provide me with an estimated timeline for completion and any official documentation of the delay for our records?"

Cuando los problemas podrían resultar en multas significativas: "Given the serious nature of this situation, I would like to contact my company's legal department to ensure we handle this appropriately. Could you please provide information about the specific violations being alleged and the appeals process?"

Para situaciones que requieren coordinación con múltiples agencias: "This issue appears to involve multiple regulatory agencies. Could you help me understand which agencies are involved and who I should contact to resolve each aspect of the problem?"

Manteniendo Relaciones Profesionales Durante Crisis

Incluso en las situaciones más frustrantes, mantener el profesionalismo puede influenciar positivamente el resultado.

Cuando expreses frustración, hazlo de manera constructiva: "I understand that everyone is doing their job, and I appreciate the thoroughness of the inspection process. However, the delays are creating significant business impacts, and I'm hoping we can find a way to resolve this efficiently."

Para agradecer la cooperación incluso durante problemas: "I want to thank you for your patience and professionalism in handling this complex situation. I understand that these issues can be as frustrating for you as they are for me."

Al documentar problemas para futura referencia: "For our records and to help prevent similar issues in the future, could you provide me with information about what specifically caused this problem and what we might do differently next time?"

La resolución efectiva de problemas fronterizos no se trata de evitar todos los problemas, que es imposible en un sistema tan complejo, sino de manejar los problemas que surgen de manera profesional, eficiente, y con el mínimo impacto en tu negocio y relaciones comerciales.

Capítulo 3: Inglés para Almacenes y Muelles de Carga

La mala comunicación en muelles de carga representa el 34% de todos los reclamos por daños de carga, costando a la industria $1.8 mil millones anuales. Esta cifra no incluye los costos ocultos de tiempo perdido, relaciones comerciales dañadas, y oportunidades de negocio perdidas cuando los conductores no pueden comunicarse efectivamente con el personal de almacén. En un mundo donde las operaciones de almacén funcionan con cronogramas ajustados y tolerancias mínimas de error, la capacidad de comunicarse claramente en inglés puede ser la diferencia entre una operación fluida y un desastre logístico.

Los almacenes modernos operan como ecosistemas complejos donde cada elemento, desde la llegada del camión hasta la descarga final, debe coordinarse con precisión militar. Una comunicación deficiente en cualquier punto de este proceso puede crear un efecto dominó que afecta no solo tu entrega, sino las operaciones de todo el día. Para los conductores profesionales, dominar la comunicación en inglés para almacenes no es solo una habilidad útil, es una competencia esencial que determina su eficiencia, reputación, y éxito económico.

Este capítulo te equipará con las herramientas lingüísticas específicas para navegar los entornos de almacén más complejos, desde mega-centros de distribución hasta pequeñas operaciones especializadas, asegurando que puedas comunicarte con autoridad y precisión sin importar cuán compleja sea la situación logística.

3.1 Comunicación de Registro y Programación

La Danza Compleja de la Coordinación de Almacén

Los almacenes modernos funcionan como sinfonías logísticas donde cada movimiento debe estar sincronizado con precisión. Tu llegada no es simplemente un evento aislado; es un componente crítico en una cadena de operaciones que incluye programación de personal, disponibilidad de equipamiento, coordinación de inventario, y optimización de espacio. Entender esta complejidad te permite comunicarte de manera que facilite, en lugar de complicar, las operaciones del almacén.

La comunicación efectiva comienza antes de que llegues al almacén. Los sistemas modernos de gestión de almacenes dependen de información precisa sobre horarios de llegada para optimizar recursos y minimizar tiempos de espera. Cuando esta información es inexacta o está mal comunicada, crea ineficiencias que se propagan a través de toda la operación.

Anunciando Llegada y Confirmando Horarios de Cita

La primera impresión que das al personal de almacén establece el tono para toda tu visita. Los gerentes de muelle han desarrollado la capacidad de evaluar rápidamente la competencia de un conductor basándose en cómo se presenta y comunica durante los primeros minutos de interacción.

Cuando te acerques al escritorio de registro o caseta de seguridad, tu comunicación inicial debe ser profesional, clara, y completa. Una presentación efectiva incluye identificación personal, información de la compañía, y detalles específicos sobre tu cita: "Good morning, I'm [tu nombre] from [nombre de la compañía]. I have a [pickup/delivery] appointment scheduled for [hora específica] under appointment number [número]. I'm driving truck number [número] with trailer [número]."

Esta presentación proporciona toda la información crítica que el personal necesita para procesar tu llegada rápidamente. Incluir el número de cita es particularmente importante porque muchos almacenes manejan cientos de citas diarias, y el número de cita es la clave principal en sus sistemas de gestión.

Si llegaste temprano, la comunicación sobre este hecho debe ser estratégica. Llegar temprano puede ser una ventaja o un problema, dependiendo de las operaciones del almacén. Una aproximación efectiva es: "I know my appointment isn't until [hora], but I arrived early and wanted to check in to see if there's any possibility of being serviced earlier, or if you'd prefer I wait until my scheduled time."

Esta comunicación demuestra respeto por el cronograma del almacén mientras expresas disponibilidad para flexibilidad que podría beneficiar a ambas partes. Algunos almacenes pueden acomodar llegadas tempranas si tienen capacidad disponible, mientras que otros operan con cronogramas estrictos que no permiten desviaciones.

Para confirmación de horarios, especialmente cuando has experimentado retrasos en ruta, la comunicación proactiva es esencial: "I wanted to confirm my appointment for [hora]. I've experienced some delays and I'm currently [ubicación] with an estimated arrival time of [hora revisada]. Will this create any problems with my slot, or do I need to reschedule?"

Esta comunicación permite al almacén hacer ajustes necesarios en su programación y demuestra tu profesionalismo en manejar cambios de cronograma.

Entendiendo Asignaciones de Bahías y Procedimientos Específicos

Los almacenes operan con sistemas específicos de asignación de bahías que pueden basarse en tipo de carga, equipamiento requerido, secuencia de operaciones, o disponibilidad de personal. Entender estos sistemas y poder comunicarte efectivamente sobre ellos acelera significativamente tu procesamiento.

Cuando recibas una asignación de bahía, confirma la información específicamente: "You've assigned me to dock door [número]. Should I proceed directly there, or are there any specific procedures I need to follow first?" Esta pregunta demuestra que entiendes que diferentes almacenes tienen diferentes protocolos de llegada.

Algunos almacenes requieren inspecciones de seguridad antes del acoplamiento: "I understand I need to complete a safety inspection before docking. Where should I report for this inspection, and what documentation do I need to bring?" Esta comunicación muestra conciencia de los procedimientos de seguridad y disposición para cumplir.

Para operaciones que requieren equipamiento especial, como montacargas específicos o equipos de manejo de materiales, la comunicación debe incluir verificación de disponibilidad: "My load requires [tipo específico de equipamiento] for unloading. I want to confirm that this equipment is available and that the dock assignment is appropriate for this type of operation."

Los procedimientos específicos del almacén pueden incluir requirements únicos de documentación, secuencias de descarga particulares, o protocolos de seguridad especializados. Una pregunta efectiva es: "Are there any specific procedures unique to this facility that I should be aware of? I want to make sure I follow all your requirements correctly."

Cuando los almacenes manejan múltiples tipos de operaciones simultáneamente, es importante entender dónde encaja tu carga en sus prioridades: "I'm delivering [tipo de carga]. Is there anything special about how this type of delivery is handled here, or any timing considerations I should be aware of?"

Comunicando Retrasos y Cambios de Cronograma

Los retrasos son inevitables en el transporte por carretera, pero la manera en que comunicas estos retrasos puede minimizar su impacto en las operaciones del almacén y mantener relaciones comerciales positivas.

La comunicación temprana sobre retrasos potenciales es crucial: "I'm currently experiencing delays due to [razón específica] and wanted to give you advance notice that I may be late for my [hora] appointment. My current estimated arrival time is [hora revisada]. How would you like me to handle this situation?"

Esta comunicación proporciona información específica sobre el retraso y solicita orientación sobre cómo proceder, demostrando respeto por las operaciones del almacén y disposición para trabajar cooperativamente para minimizar el impacto.

Para retrasos causados por condiciones externas como clima o tráfico: "I'm delayed due to weather conditions on [ruta específica]. I'm monitoring the situation closely and will provide updates as my estimated arrival time becomes more certain. Is there flexibility in my appointment time, or should I look at rescheduling?"

Cuando los retrasos son causados por problemas mecánicos: "I've experienced a mechanical issue that required emergency repair. The repair is complete, but I'm now [tiempo] behind schedule. I understand this affects your planning, and I'm prepared to work with whatever arrangement works best for your operations."

Para retrasos en instalaciones anteriores: "I was delayed at my previous stop due to [razón específica]. This was beyond my control, and I have documentation of the delay if needed. I want to work with you to minimize any impact on your operations."

Solicitando Carga Prioritaria y Manejar Urgencias

Las situaciones que requieren manejo prioritario necesitan comunicación especialmente hábil que equilibre urgencia con respeto por las operaciones existentes del almacén.

Cuando transportas carga verdaderamente urgente, la comunicación inicial debe establecer claramente la naturaleza de la urgencia: "I have an urgent shipment that needs priority handling due to [razón específica]. I understand this may disrupt your normal schedule, and I'm prepared to work with whatever accommodations you can make."

Para cargas médicas o de emergencia: "I'm carrying medical supplies that are needed urgently at [destino]. The shipment is time-critical for patient care. Is there any way to expedite the loading/unloading process while maintaining all safety requirements?"

Las situaciones de just-in-time manufacturing requieren explicaciones técnicas: "This delivery is for a just-in-time production line that's scheduled to begin at [tiempo específico]. Any delay beyond [tiempo límite] would shut down production. I know this creates pressure on your operations, and I'm willing to assist in any way that might speed up the process."

Cuando la urgencia está relacionada con condiciones de la carga: "I'm carrying perishable goods that are approaching their temperature tolerance limits. While I don't want to disrupt your schedule, the product quality depends on quick processing. What options do we have for expediting this delivery?"

Para situaciones donde tu cronograma personal crea urgencia, la comunicación debe ser honesta pero profesional: "I have a legal hours-of-service situation that requires me to complete this delivery and reach a rest area within [tiempo]. I understand my poor planning shouldn't become your emergency, but I wanted to explain the situation in case there's any flexibility possible."

Navegando Sistemas de Gestión de Citas Complejos

Los almacenes modernos frecuentemente utilizan sistemas de gestión de citas sofisticados que requieren interacciones específicas para funcionar eficientemente.

Cuando tengas dificultades con sistemas automatizados de check-in: "I'm having trouble with the automated check-in system. Could someone assist me with the process, or is there an alternative way to register my arrival?"

Para cambios de último minuto en sistemas de citas: "I need to modify my appointment due to [razón]. Is this something I can do through your system, or do I need to work with someone directly to make the change?"

Cuando los sistemas muestren información conflictiva: "Your system shows [información], but my paperwork shows [información diferente]. Could we verify which information is correct to avoid any confusion during loading/unloading?"

Estableciendo Expectativas de Tiempo y Comunicación Continua

El manejo efectivo de expectativas sobre timing es crucial para mantener relaciones positivas y operaciones eficientes.

Para operaciones de descarga complejas: "Based on the type and quantity of cargo I'm delivering, what's your typical timeframe for this type of operation? I want to plan my schedule accordingly and communicate accurate information to my dispatcher."

Cuando necesites actualizaciones de progreso: "I have additional stops planned for today and need to provide accurate timing to my next customer. Could you give me periodic updates on how the loading/unloading is progressing?"

Para coordinación con múltiples partes: "I know several people are involved in processing this shipment. Who should I check with for status updates, and how often would be appropriate to inquire about progress?"

La comunicación efectiva en almacenes requiere una comprensión sofisticada de operaciones logísticas complejas combinada con habilidades interpersonales que faciliten cooperación y eficiencia. Cada interacción es una oportunidad de demostrar profesionalismo y construir relaciones que facilitarán operaciones futuras más fluidas.

3.2 Verificación de Carga y Documentación

La verificación precisa de carga representa uno de los aspectos más críticos de las operaciones de almacén, donde los errores pueden propagarse a través de toda la cadena de suministro causando problemas financieros y operacionales significativos. Para los conductores profesionales, la capacidad de comunicarse efectivamente durante estos procesos de verificación no solo protege tu responsabilidad personal, sino que también contribuye a la integridad de toda la operación logística.

Conteos de Piezas y Verificación de Inventario

Los conteos de piezas en almacenes modernos involucran múltiples niveles de verificación que van desde conteos básicos hasta verificaciones detalladas de códigos de producto, números de lote, y especificaciones técnicas. Tu papel como conductor incluye participar activamente en estos procesos de verificación para asegurar precisión antes de que la carga salga del almacén.

Cuando participes en conteos de carga, la comunicación debe ser específica y verificable. En lugar de simplemente confirmar que "everything looks good," tu comunicación debe incluir detalles específicos: "I count [número específico] pallets being loaded, which matches the bill of lading quantity. Each pallet appears to contain [descripción específica] as described in the shipping documentation."

Para cargas que incluyen múltiples códigos de producto o referencias de inventario, la verificación debe ser sistemática: "I'm verifying the load contents against the pick list. I see [cantidad] units of item [código de producto], [cantidad] units of item [código de producto], and so forth. The quantities match the documentation, and I don't see any obvious substitutions or wrong items."

Los conteos parciales, donde solo una porción de tu carga se origina en una instalación específica, requieren comunicación especialmente clara: "This is a partial load pickup. According to the documentation, I should be receiving [cantidad específica] pallets from this location, which will be combined with [cantidad] pallets I picked up at [ubicación anterior]. The total final count should be [cantidad total] pallets."

Cuando identifiques discrepancias durante el conteo, la comunicación inmediata es crucial: "I'm showing a discrepancy in the count. The bill of lading indicates [cantidad], but I'm only counting [cantidad actual]. Could we recount this together to verify the actual quantity being loaded?"

Números de Pallets y Sistemas de Rastreo

Los sistemas modernos de gestión de almacenes dependen de números únicos de pallets y códigos de rastreo para mantener precisión en el inventario y rastreabilidad en la cadena de suministro. Tu comprensión y comunicación sobre estos sistemas puede prevenir problemas significativos downstream.

Los números de pallets deben verificarse tanto individualmente como en conjunto: "I'm documenting the pallet numbers for this shipment. The pallets are numbered [lista de números], and I want to confirm these match your records before departure." Esta verificación es especialmente importante para shipments de alto valor o productos regulados donde la rastreabilidad es legalmente requerida.

Para operaciones que utilizan códigos de barras o etiquetas RFID, tu comunicación debe confirmar que el sistema de rastreo está funcionando correctamente: "I notice that some pallets have barcode labels while others don't. Should all pallets have tracking labels for this shipment, or is this normal for this type of cargo?"

Los sistemas de intercambio de pallets requieren comunicación específica sobre responsabilidades: "I understand this shipment involves a pallet exchange. I'm delivering [cantidad] pallets and should receive [cantidad] empty pallets in return. What's the procedure for documenting this exchange, and who verifies the condition of the returned pallets?"

Distribución de Peso y Cumplimiento Legal

La distribución adecuada del peso no es solo una cuestión de cumplimiento legal; también afecta la seguridad en carretera, el desgaste del vehículo, y la estabilidad de la carga durante el tránsito.

Cuando discutas distribución de peso con personal de almacén, tu comunicación debe incluir limitaciones específicas de tu equipamiento: "My trailer has a capacity de carga de [peso] pounds, and I need to maintain proper weight distribution. The heaviest items should be loaded [ubicación específica] to maintain balance and stay within axle weight limits."

Para cargas que se acercan a límites de peso, la verificación proactiva es esencial: "This appears to be a heavy load. Could we verify the total weight before completing the loading? I want to make sure we stay within legal limits and that the weight is distributed properly for safe transportation."

Los shipments que requieren distribución específica de peso debido a la naturaleza de la mercancía necesitan comunicación técnica: "I understand this equipment is weight-sensitive and needs to be positioned [ubicación específica] in the trailer. Could we verify the placement before securing the load to ensure it meets both transportation requirements and product specifications?"

Reportando Daños y Discrepancias

La documentación precisa de daños y discrepancias protege todas las partes involucradas en la transacción y proporciona la base para resolución de reclamos futuros.

Cuando identifiques mercancía dañada durante la carga, la comunicación debe ser inmediata y específica: "I'm seeing damage to [descripción específica de items]. The damage appears to be [descripción del daño] and affects [cantidad o porcentaje]. Should we document this damage before loading, or do you prefer to handle damaged items separately?"

Para artículos faltantes, la comunicación debe distinguir entre items que nunca llegaron al almacén versus items que se perdieron durante las operaciones del almacén: "According to the pick list, I should receive [cantidad] units of [producto específico], but I only see [cantidad actual]. Could we verify whether these items are available elsewhere in the warehouse or if there's a shortage from the original inventory?"

Las discrepancias en especificaciones de producto requieren verificación cuidadosa: "The bill of lading specifies [especificación], but the items being loaded appear to be [especificación diferente]. Could we verify which specification is correct, or determine if this substitution is authorized by the customer?"

Terminología de Almacén y Operaciones Especializadas

El dominio de terminología especializada de almacén te permite comunicarte efectivamente con personal experimentado y entender operaciones complejas que afectan tu carga.

Las operaciones de cross-dock requieren comprensión de timing y flujo: "I understand this is a cross-dock operation where my inbound cargo will be transferred directly to outbound trucks. What's the typical timeframe for this process, and where should I position my trailer to facilitate the transfer?"

Para shipments LTL (Less Than Truckload), la comunicación debe abordar múltiples entregas: "This is an LTL shipment with stops at [lista de ubicaciones]. The freight for each stop should be accessible in delivery sequence. Could we verify that the load is organized for efficient unloading at each destination?"

Los envíos ciegos, donde el destinatario final no debe conocer el origen real de la mercancía, requieren comunicación cuidadosa sobre documentación: "I understand this is a blind shipment. What documentation should I present at delivery, and is there any information I should not disclose to the receiving party?"

Las operaciones de consolidación involucran combining múltiples shipments: "This appears to be a consolidation load where I'm picking up freight from multiple shippers for delivery to a single destination. Could you help me understand how the freight should be organized in the trailer to facilitate unloading at the final destination?"

Capítulo 4: Inglés Mecánico y de Mantenimiento

El camionero promedio experimenta 2.5 averías por año, con 60% ocurriendo en áreas donde no hay mecánicos hispanohablantes disponibles. Esta estadística representa más que simples números; representa horas perdidas en carretera, costos de reparación inflados debido a malentendidos, y la frustración de intentar explicar problemas complejos en un idioma técnico que puede determinar si recibes la reparación correcta o te cobran por servicios innecesarios.

La comunicación mecánica efectiva trasciende el simple intercambio de información; es la diferencia entre una reparación de $200 que resuelve el problema real y una "reparación" de $2,000 que no aborda la causa raíz porque el mecánico nunca entendió completamente qué estaba mal. En el mundo del mantenimiento vehicular, la precisión del lenguaje técnico puede literalmente salvar vidas, prevenir accidentes catastróficos, y proteger tu inversión en equipamiento.

Los talleres mecánicos operan en un ambiente donde el tiempo es dinero y los malentendidos son costosos. Cuando puedes comunicarte con precisión técnica sobre problemas mecánicos, no solo aceleras el proceso de diagnóstico, sino que también estableces credibilidad profesional que resulta en mejor servicio y precios más justos. Este capítulo te equipará con el vocabulario técnico y las estrategias de comunicación necesarias para interactuar efectivamente con mecánicos, diagnosticar problemas con precisión, y asegurar que tu vehículo reciba exactamente el mantenimiento que necesita.

4.1 Describir Problemas Mecánicos

La Anatomía de la Comunicación Técnica Efectiva

La descripción efectiva de problemas mecánicos requiere una comprensión fundamental de la diferencia entre síntomas observables y diagnósticos técnicos. Los mecánicos experimentados están entrenados para identificar patrones específicos en las descripciones de problemas que los guían hacia diagnósticos precisos. Tu capacidad para proporcionar esta información de manera sistemática y técnicamente precisa puede reducir dramáticamente el tiempo de diagnóstico y prevenir reparaciones innecesarias.

Los sistemas mecánicos de vehículos comerciales son interdependientes, y un problema en un sistema frecuentemente se manifiesta como síntomas en otros sistemas. Esta complejidad significa que tu descripción debe ser comprehensiva, secuencial, y basada en observaciones objetivas en lugar de interpretaciones subjetivas.

Vocabulario Técnico para Sistemas de Motor

El motor de un vehículo comercial es un sistema complejo donde múltiples subsistemas trabajan en conjunto para generar potencia. Cuando experimentes problemas relacionados con el motor, tu descripción debe incluir información específica sobre rendimiento, sonidos, temperaturas, y comportamiento bajo diferentes condiciones operacionales.

Para problemas de rendimiento del motor, la descripción debe incluir condiciones específicas donde ocurren los síntomas. "The engine is losing power when climbing hills under load" proporciona información específica sobre cuándo y cómo se manifiesta el problema. Esta descripción es significativamente más útil que simplemente decir "the engine doesn't have power" porque indica que el problema está relacionado con carga y pendientes, sugiriendo posibles problemas con inyección de combustible, turboalimentación, o restricciones de admisión de aire.

Los sonidos del motor requieren descripción técnica específica porque diferentes tipos de ruidos indican problemas específicos. "There's a knocking sound from the engine that gets worse under acceleration and is most noticeable when the engine is warm" describe un patrón específico que sugiere problemas de combustión o desgaste interno. Comparativamente, "There's a high-pitched whining noise that increases with RPM but doesn't change with load" sugiere problemas con componentes rotativos como alternadores, bombas de agua, o ventiladores.

Las temperaturas operacionales proporcionan información crítica sobre la salud del motor. "The engine temperature gauge reads normal, but I'm seeing white steam from the exhaust stack, especially when the engine is cold" describe síntomas específicos que podrían indicar problemas de refrigerante interno sin sobrecalentamiento aparente.

Los problemas de arranque requieren descripción detallada de la secuencia de eventos. "The engine cranks normally but won't start. I can hear the fuel pump running, and there's no unusual smoke from the exhaust during cranking attempts" proporciona información específica sobre sistemas eléctricos, combustible, y compresión que ayuda a los mecánicos a enfocar su diagnóstico.

Para problemas de consumo de combustible, la descripción debe incluir datos cuantitativos cuando sea posible: "My fuel economy has dropped from [MPG normal] to [MPG actual] over the past [período de tiempo]. This change coincided with [cualquier evento específico como mantenimiento reciente o cambio de rutas]."

Los problemas del sistema de escape requieren descripción de color, cantidad, y timing del humo: "There's heavy black smoke during acceleration that clears up once I reach cruising speed. The smoke is most noticeable when accelerating from a stop or climbing hills." Esta descripción indica problemas específicos de combustión que se manifiestan bajo carga.

Sistemas de Transmisión y Comunicación Técnica

La transmisión de un vehículo comercial es responsable de transferir potencia del motor a las ruedas mientras proporciona múltiples relaciones de engranajes para optimizar rendimiento bajo diferentes condiciones. Los problemas de transmisión pueden manifestarse como problemas de cambio, ruidos, vibraciones, o pérdida de potencia.

Los problemas de cambio requieren descripción específica de cuándo y cómo ocurren: "The transmission is slipping out of [gear específico] under load, especially when climbing hills. It shifts normally into the gear, but then loses engagement and revs up without transferring power to the wheels." Esta descripción proporciona información específica sobre sincronización, engagement, y condiciones de carga que ayudan al diagnóstico.

Para transmisiones automáticas, la descripción debe incluir comportamiento durante diferentes fases de operación: "The transmission shifts normally through all gears when cold, but once it warms up, it hesitates between [gear específico] and [gear específico], and sometimes refuses to shift up from [gear específico] even when I reach appropriate speed."

Los sonidos de transmisión requieren descripción técnica que incluya cuándo ocurren en relación con la operación del vehículo: "There's a grinding noise that only occurs when shifting from [gear específico] to [gear específico]. The noise doesn't happen with other gear changes, and it's worse when the transmission is cold."

Las vibraciones relacionadas con la transmisión deben describirse en términos de velocidad, carga, y gear: "There's a vibration that starts at approximately [velocidad] and gets worse as speed increases. The vibration is most noticeable in [gear específico] and seems to come from the center of the truck rather than the wheels."

Los problemas del embrague requieren descripción de engagement, travel del pedal, y behavior under load: "The clutch pedal travel feels normal, but the clutch is slipping under heavy acceleration or when starting on hills. The slipping is getting progressively worse and is now noticeable even during normal acceleration."

Sistemas de Frenos y Terminología Crítica de Seguridad

Los sistemas de frenos representan el aspecto más crítico de seguridad de tu vehículo, y los problemas de frenos requieren comunicación inmediata y técnicamente precisa. Los mecánicos necesitan entender exactamente qué está experimentando el sistema de frenos para priorizar apropiadamente las reparaciones y asegurar seguridad.

Para problemas de efectividad de frenado, la descripción debe incluir distancias, pedal feel, y behavior bajo diferentes condiciones: "The braking distance has increased noticeably, especially when the truck is loaded. The brake pedal feels spongy and goes farther to the floor than normal before the brakes engage effectively."

Los sonidos de frenos proporcionan información diagnóstica específica: "There's a grinding noise from the front wheels during braking that gets worse as I apply more pressure. The noise doesn't occur when I'm not braking, and it seems to be coming from the [ubicación específica]."

Los problemas del sistema de aire de frenos requieren descripción técnica de presiones, tiempos, y behavior: "The air pressure builds to normal operating pressure, but it takes longer than usual. Once at pressure, the system holds pressure normally, but I notice the compressor is cycling more frequently than normal."

Para problemas de brake fade, la descripción debe incluir condiciones específicas: "After extended downhill braking, the brakes become less effective and the pedal goes further to the floor. The problem improves after the brakes cool down, but it's happening more frequently than it used to."

Los problemas de parking brake requieren descripción de engagement y holding power: "The parking brake sets normally and holds the truck when it's empty, but it doesn't seem to hold effectively when the truck is loaded, especially on inclines."

Distinguiendo Entre Síntomas y Causas

Una de las habilidades más importantes en comunicación mecánica es la capacidad de describir lo que observas sin diagnosticar prematuramente la causa. Los mecánicos experimentados prefieren síntomas objetivos a diagnósticos amateur porque los síntomas les permiten aplicar su experiencia profesional al diagnóstico.

Cuando el vehículo "jala hacia la derecha," esta es una descripción precisa del síntoma. Decir que tienes "un problema de alineación" es un diagnóstico prematuro que podría ser incorrecto. El jalón hacia la derecha podría ser causado por alineación, pero también podría ser causado por diferencias de presión de llantas, desgaste irregular de llantas, problemas de frenos, o problemas de suspensión.

La descripción efectiva del síntoma sería: "The truck pulls consistently to the right, especially at highway speeds. The pulling is noticeable when I'm driving straight and becomes worse when I release my grip on the steering wheel. The pulling doesn't seem to be affected by braking or acceleration."

Para problemas de vibración, describir el síntoma sería: "There's a vibration that I feel through the steering wheel that starts at about 55 mph and gets worse as speed increases. The vibration is consistent and doesn't change when I brake or accelerate." Diagnosticar esto como "wheel balance problem" limita las opciones de diagnóstico del mecánico.

Los sonidos deben describirse en términos de características observables: "There's a rhythmic thumping sound that increases in frequency as speed increases. The sound seems to come from the rear of the truck and is most noticeable on smooth pavement." Esta descripción es más útil que diagnosticar esto como "a bad tire" porque el sonido podría ser causado por llantas, but también por problemas de bearing, brake, o suspensión.

Comunicando Niveles de Urgencia y Preocupaciones de Seguridad

La comunicación efectiva sobre urgency y safety requiere una comprensión de cómo los mecánicos priorizan el trabajo y qué information necesitan para tomar decisiones apropiadas sobre scheduling y resource allocation.

Para problemas que afectan safety inmediata, tu comunicación debe ser directa e include specific safety concerns: "I have a brake problem that I consider a safety emergency. The brake pedal is going to the floor and the stopping distance has increased dramatically. I don't feel safe continuing to drive this vehicle without immediate attention."

Los problemas que afectan reliability pero no immediate safety requieren different communication: "I'm experiencing a problem that's getting progressively worse and I'm concerned it could leave me stranded. The issue is [descripción específica] and it's happening more frequently. While it's not immediately dangerous, I don't want to risk a breakdown in a remote area."

Para problems que affect efficiency pero no safety o reliability: "I have a performance issue that's affecting my fuel economy and operational efficiency. While the truck is safe to drive, the problem is costing me money and I'd like to address it at your earliest convenience."

La communication sobre previous attempts at repair require specific information: "This problem was previously diagnosed as [diagnóstico anterior] at [ubicación] and they replaced [componentes]. However, the problem persists and may actually be getting worse. I'm wondering if there might be an underlying issue that wasn't addressed."

When communicating about intermittent problems: "This is an intermittent problem that doesn't happen consistently. It typically occurs [condiciones específicas] and lasts for [duración]. While it's not happening right now, I'm concerned about it getting worse or causing a breakdown when I least expect it."

La comunicación mecánica efectiva is fundamentally about building a bridge between your observational experience as a professional driver and the technical expertise of professional mechanics. When you can describe problems with precision, communicate urgency appropriately, and distinguish between symptoms and causes, you create conditions for efficient, accurate, and cost-effective repairs que keep you safely on the road.

4.2 Entender Estimados de Reparación y Tiempos

La navegación efectiva de estimados de reparación representa una de las habilidades comerciales más críticas para conductores profesionales, donde la diferencia entre negociación informada y aceptación pasiva puede significar miles de dólares en costos innecesarios a lo largo de una carrera. Los talleres mecánicos operan como negocios complejos con estructuras de precios que incluyen costos de mano de obra, markup de partes, overhead, y márgenes de ganancia que no siempre son transparentes para el consumidor promedio.

Decodificando la Estructura de Estimados de Reparación

Los estimados de reparación modernos contienen información técnica y financiera que requiere comprensión sofisticada para evaluar apropiadamente. Cuando un mecánico presenta un estimado, tu respuesta inicial establece el tono para toda la negociación y determina si recibes explicaciones detalladas o simplemente una cifra final que debes aceptar o rechazar.

Una aproximación efectiva para revisar estimados comienza con solicitar desglose detallado: "I'd like to understand the breakdown of this estimate. Could you walk me through the labor hours, parts costs, and any additional charges so I can understand what each component of the repair involves?" Esta solicitud demuestra conocimiento comercial y establece expectativas de transparencia.

Para reparaciones complejas que involucran múltiples sistemas, la comunicación debe abordar priorización: "This estimate covers several different issues. Could you help me understand which repairs are critical for safety and operation versus which ones could be delayed if necessary? I want to prioritize based on both urgency and budget considerations."

Los estimados frecuentemente incluyen trabajo de diagnóstico que ya se ha completado, y entender estos costos es crucial: "I see there's a diagnostic fee included in this estimate. Since you've already identified the problem, is this fee separate from the repair cost, or is it included in the total if I authorize the work?"

Cuando los estimados parecen significativamente más altos que esperabas, la comunicación debe buscar entendimiento antes de rechazo: "This estimate is higher than I anticipated for this type of repair. Could you help me understand what factors are contributing to the cost? Are there complications specific to my vehicle, or additional work that became necessary during diagnosis?"

Inglés para camioneros

Negociando Costos y Entendiendo Términos de Garantía

La negociación efectiva de costos de reparación requiere una comprensión de los factores que los talleres pueden y no pueden controlar, junto con estrategias de comunicación que buscan valor en lugar de simplemente precio más bajo.

Los costos de mano de obra a menudo tienen menos flexibilidad que otros componentes, pero entender estos costos ayuda en la negociación: "I understand that labor rates are generally fixed, but I'm wondering about the number of hours estimated for this job. Is this based on book time, or actual time you expect it to take? If the job takes less time than estimated, would that be reflected in the final cost?"

Para talleres que han proporcionado buen servicio previamente, la lealtad del cliente puede ser un factor de negociación: "I've been bringing my trucks here for [período de tiempo] and have always been satisfied with the work. Given our ongoing relationship, is there any flexibility in the pricing, or are there ways to structure the work to reduce costs?"

Los términos de garantía requieren discusión específica antes de autorizar trabajo: "What warranty do you provide on this repair? Does the warranty cover both parts and labor, and what's the time period? If I have problems related to this repair while I'm on the road, how do you handle warranty work?"

Las garantías de partes versus garantías de mano de obra tienen diferentes implicaciones: "I want to understand the difference between the parts warranty and your labor warranty. If a part fails under warranty but I'm in a different state, can I have the part replaced elsewhere and still maintain the warranty coverage?"

Para reparaciones mayores, las garantías extendidas pueden ser opciones: "For a repair of this magnitude, do you offer extended warranty options? What would be the cost difference, and what additional coverage would that provide?"

Explorando Opciones de Partes y Alternativas de Costo

El mercado de partes para vehículos comerciales incluye múltiples niveles de calidad y precio, desde partes OEM hasta opciones remanufacturadas y aftermarket. Entender estas opciones y poder discutirlas efectivamente puede resultar en ahorros significativos sin comprometer calidad.

Las partes OEM representan el estándar más alto pero también el costo más alto: "You've quoted OEM parts for this repair. While I understand these are the highest quality, what are the alternatives? Are there aftermarket parts that would provide similar performance at lower cost?"

Las partes remanufacturadas ofrecen un balance entre costo y calidad: "I'm interested in learning about remanufactured parts for this repair. What's the quality difference compared to new parts, and what kind of warranty do remanufactured parts carry?"

Para componentes donde la calidad es crítica para seguridad: "I understand that some components shouldn't be compromised on quality. For this repair, which parts would you strongly recommend staying with OEM, and which ones could safely use alternative options?"

Los arreglos temporales pueden ser opciones para situaciones financieras difíciles: "Given my current situation, I need to get back on the road but may not be able to afford the complete repair right now. Is there a temporary fix that would be safe for operation while I arrange financing for the permanent repair?"

Las partes usadas representan la opción de menor costo pero requieren evaluación cuidadosa: "Are quality used parts available for this repair? If so, what kind of inspection do you do on used parts, and what warranty would they carry?"

Autorizando Reparaciones y Estableciendo Términos de Pago

La autorización de reparaciones involucra más que simplemente decir "yes" a un estimado. La comunicación efectiva durante esta fase protege tus intereses financieros y asegura entendimiento claro de expectativas mutuas.

Para autorización de trabajo, la comunicación debe ser específica y documentada: "I'm authorizing the repair work as outlined in estimate number [número] for a total cost of [cantidad]. This authorization is based on the understanding that any additional work discovered during the repair will be discussed with me before proceeding."

Los términos de pago deben establecerse claramente: "What are your payment terms for this repair? Do you require payment upon completion, or do you offer financing options? If additional work becomes necessary, how would that affect payment timing?"

Para reparaciones que podrían exceder el estimado original: "I understand that sometimes additional problems are discovered during repair. What's your policy for cost overruns? At what point would you contact me for additional authorization, and what happens if I can't be reached immediately?"

Las garantías de tiempo de completión son importantes para conductores comerciales: "When do you expect this repair to be completed? If there are delays beyond your control, what's your communication policy for keeping customers informed?"

Manejando Cambios Durante la Reparación

Los cambios durante la reparación son comunes en trabajos mecánicos complejos, y tu comunicación sobre estos cambios puede prevenir sorpresas financieras y disputas.

Cuando los mecánicos descubren problemas adicionales: "I understand you've found additional problems during the repair. Could you explain what you've discovered, how it relates to the original problem, and what the cost implications are? I need to understand whether this additional work is necessary for safe operation or if it can be deferred."

Para situaciones donde las partes ordenadas no están disponibles: "I understand the parts you ordered aren't available immediately. What are my options? Can you source alternative parts, or would it be better to wait for the original parts? How would each option affect timing and cost?"

Cuando el trabajo toma más tiempo que estimado: "I know the repair is taking longer than originally estimated. Can you help me understand what's causing the delay and provide a realistic timeline for completion? This affects my ability to meet commitments to customers."

Capítulo 5: Comunicación con Despachador y Gestión de Flota

La comunicación clara conductor-despachador aumenta las tasas de entrega a tiempo en 23% y reduce las millas vacías en 15%. Estas estadísticas representan la diferencia entre una operación de transporte rentable y una que lucha constantemente con ineficiencias costosas. En un mundo donde cada milla cuenta y cada retraso se traduce en dinero perdido, la calidad de comunicación entre conductores y despachadores determina directamente el éxito económico de toda la operación.

Los despachadores modernos manejan información compleja de múltiples conductores simultáneamente, coordinando entregas, gestionando emergencias, y optimizando rutas en tiempo real. Para ellos, la comunicación efectiva no es solo conveniencia; es la herramienta fundamental que les permite tomar decisiones informadas que afectan la rentabilidad de toda la flota. Cuando un conductor puede comunicarse de manera clara, concisa, y profesional, se convierte en un partner estratégico en lugar de simplemente un empleado que necesita dirección constante.

La comunicación efectiva con despachadores trasciende el simple intercambio de información. Es sobre construir relaciones profesionales que resultan en mejores asignaciones de carga, mayor flexibilidad en programación, y support durante situaciones difíciles. Los conductores que dominan esta comunicación frecuentemente reciben preferencia para las cargas más deseables, obtienen assistance rápida cuando enfrentan problemas, y desarrollan reputaciones que abren puertas a oportunidades mejor remuneradas.

Este capítulo te equipará con las habilidades de comunicación específicas necesarias para establecer relaciones profesionales sólidas con despachadores, optimizar tu eficiencia operacional, y posicionarte como un conductor confiable que contribuye al éxito de toda la organización.

5.1 Reportes Diarios y Actualizaciones de Estado

La Arquitectura de la Comunicación Profesional con Despachadores

Los despachadores operan en un ambiente de alta presión donde deben tomar decisiones rápidas basadas en información que reciben de múltiples fuentes. Tu comunicación debe ser estructurada de manera que proporcione exactamente la información que necesitan para tomar estas decisiones de manera eficiente. La comunicación efectiva no es simplemente sobre transmitir datos; es about providing context que permite decision-making informado.

Los sistemas modernos de dispatching integran múltiples fuentes de información incluyendo GPS tracking, traffic data, customer requirements, y regulatory constraints. Sin embargo, estos sistemas no pueden capturar completely la realidad operacional que experimentas en la carretera. Tu comunicación verbal proporciona el context humano que transforma data en intelligence actionable.

Reportando Ubicación y Actualizaciones de ETA de Manera Profesional

La comunicación de ubicación efectiva va mucho más allá de simplemente stating where estás. Los despachadores necesitan information que les permita assess progress, anticipar potential delays, y make proactive decisions about scheduling y customer communication.

Cuando reportes tu ubicación, la información debe ser specific y contextual: "I'm currently at mile marker 247 on I-75 northbound, approximately 15 miles south of the Georgia-Tennessee state line. I'm maintaining good speed and expect to cross into Tennessee in about 20 minutes based on current traffic conditions." Esta comunicación proporciona not only precise location sino también trajectory y timing expectations.

Para updates de ETA, la comunicación debe include factors que affect timing: "My original ETA for the Nashville delivery was 14:00, but I'm running about 30 minutes ahead of schedule due to lighter than expected traffic through Atlanta. My revised ETA is 13:30, and I wanted to give you advance notice in case this affects scheduling at the receiver."

Cuando reports delays, la comunicación debe be immediate y include impact assessment: "I'm experiencing significant delays due to an accident closure on I-40 westbound near mile marker

150. Traffic is completely stopped, and DOT is estimating a 2-hour delay for clearance. This will push my delivery ETA from 16:00 to approximately 18:00. Should I contact the receiver directly, or would you prefer to handle customer notification?"

Los reports de progress durante long hauls deben include performance metrics: "I'm making good time on this run to Denver. I'm currently in Kansas, averaging [speed] mph with fuel economy tracking at [MPG]. Based on current performance, I should arrive 2 hours ahead of the original ETA, which would put me at the receiver Thursday morning instead of Thursday afternoon."

Comunicando Condiciones de Tráfico y Road Conditions

Los reports de traffic y road conditions proporcionan valuable intelligence que beneficia not only your current operation sino también other drivers en la fleet y future planning de routes.

Para traffic conditions, la comunicación debe be specific sobre location y impact: "I'm encountering heavy construction delays on I-95 southbound between mile markers 180 and 195. Traffic is reduced to single-lane alternating flow, adding approximately 45 minutes to travel time through this section. You may want to route other drivers around this area if possible."

Weather-related road conditions require detailed description: "Road conditions are deteriorating rapidly due to snow accumulation on I-80 westbound through Wyoming. Visibility is reduced to less than a quarter mile, and several trucks have pulled off to wait for improvement. Chain requirements are likely to be implemented soon. I'm going to find a safe place to wait until conditions improve."

Para mechanical restrictions que affect routing: "I'm approaching a bridge on Route 15 that has a posted weight limit of 80,000 pounds. My gross weight is 79,500, so I should be able to cross safely, but other drivers with heavier loads should be aware of this restriction."

Construction zones require communication about timing y impact: "There's major construction on I-10 eastbound through Phoenix with significant delays between 07:00 and 18:00. I'm planning to time my passage either early morning or evening to avoid peak construction hours. This may affect scheduling for pickups in the Phoenix area."

Communicating Availability para Additional Loads y Route Changes

Professional drivers que effectively communicate their availability for additional work position themselves para better earning opportunities y demonstrate reliability que leads para preferred treatment de dispatchers.

Cuando communicate availability after delivery, provide specific information: "I've completed delivery at the Phoenix facility and will be available for pickup at 15:00 after completing my mandatory post-delivery inspection. I have [hours remaining] of available drive time today and will be legal for a full day tomorrow after my 10-hour break."

Para partial availability, be clear about constraints: "I'm available for additional freight, but I need to be within [distance] of [location] by [time] to make my next scheduled pickup. If you have anything routing in that general direction, I could handle a short haul without affecting my committed schedule."

When discussing route modifications, provide practical input: "I see you've suggested routing me through [route]. While this would work, there's an alternative routing through [alternative route] that would save approximately [distance/time] and avoid the construction delays I mentioned earlier. Would you like me to take the alternative route?"

Para emergency availability, communicate capabilities clearly: "I understand there's an urgent shipment that needs coverage. I'm currently [location] with [available hours] drive time remaining today. I could handle an emergency pickup within [radius] of my current location, but I'd need to plan my break time around the delivery schedule."

Using Transportation-Specific Codes y Abbreviations

La industria del transporte utilizes extensive coding systems y abbreviations que streamline communication y reduce ambiguity. Mastering these codes demonstrates professionalism y facilitates efficient communication.

Para equipment types, use standard industry codes: "I'm driving a 53-foot van trailer, DOT number [number], with [equipment features]. The trailer is equipped for [type] freight and has a maximum payload capacity of [weight]."

Timing communications frequently use industry-standard abbreviations: "My ETA for the consignee is 14:30 EST. I'll need approximately 2 hours for unloading based on the BOL, putting my available time for next assignment at 16:30."

Para regulatory compliance, use standard terminology: "I'm currently on line 1 (driving) with [hours] remaining on my 11-hour clock. My 14-hour clock expires at [time], and I'll need my 10-hour break starting no later than [time] to be legal for tomorrow's schedule."

HOS communications should be precise: "I took my last 10-hour break at [location] ending at [time]. I have [hours] of drive time remaining today and will be eligible for a full reset tomorrow. I'm planning my next break at [location] starting at [time]."

Load-specific codes streamline communication: "This is a team operation, and we're hauling [freight type] from [origin] to [destination]. The load is sealed with customs seal [number], and we have all required documentation for border crossing."

Building Professional Relationships Through Communication

Effective communication with dispatchers extends beyond functional information exchange to relationship building que creates mutual respect y cooperation.

When providing updates, include value-added information: "I completed delivery 30 minutes early due to efficient operations at the receiver. The receiving clerk mentioned they're always looking for reliable carriers for their regular Tuesday shipments to [destination]. This might be worth following up on for future business development."

Durante challenging situations, maintain professional tone: "I'm dealing with a mechanical issue that's going to delay my pickup by approximately 4 hours. I've arranged for repair at [location] and should be back on schedule by [time]. I understand this creates problems for scheduling, and I appreciate your patience in working through this situation."

Para performance feedback, be honest y constructive: "I noticed the pickup timing at [customer] was later than scheduled, which affected my ability to make the delivery appointment. In the future, it might be helpful to build in buffer time at this location since they seem to consistently run behind schedule."

When discussing improvements, offer solutions: "I've been thinking about ways to improve efficiency on the [route]. I've identified a fuel stop that's strategically located and offers good truck parking for breaks. Using this stop could save time and fuel costs while ensuring compliance with HOS regulations."

Managing Complex Scheduling y Multi-Stop Operations

Multi-stop operations require sophisticated communication que coordinates timing across múltiples locations y stakeholders.

Para multi-stop loads, provide comprehensive updates: "I'm currently en route to stop 2 of 4 on this multi-stop load. Stop 1 was completed on schedule at [location]. Stop 2 is scheduled for [time] at [location], and based on current progress, I expect to be on time. The remaining stops should maintain the original schedule unless unexpected delays occur."

When coordinating pickup windows, communicate constraints clearly: "The pickup at [location] has a narrow window between 08:00 and 10:00. Based on my current location and HOS status, I'll arrive at approximately 08:30, which should work well. However, if there are delays at my current stop, this timing could become tight."

Para complex routing decisions, provide operational input: "I see the planned route takes me through [city] during rush hour. Based on historical experience, this could add 2-3 hours to transit time. Would it be possible to adjust timing to avoid peak traffic, or should I plan for the additional time in my HOS calculations?"

Emergency Communication y Crisis Management

Durante emergency situations, communication must be immediate, clear, y action-oriented.

Para vehicle breakdowns, provide complete situational awareness: "I have a mechanical breakdown at mile marker [number] on [highway]. The vehicle is safely off the roadway, and I've activated emergency flashers. The problem appears to be [description], and I've contacted [service provider] for assistance. ETA for repair is [time], but this will definitely impact delivery schedules."

Durante weather emergencies, communicate safety priorities: "Weather conditions have become unsafe for continued operation. I'm shutting down at [location] for safety until conditions improve. All freight is secure, and the vehicle is parked safely. I'll provide updates on weather improvement and estimated restart time."

Para customer-related issues, maintain professional tone: "I'm experiencing issues at the delivery location. The receiver is claiming [issue], but my documentation shows [documentation]. I need guidance on how to proceed while protecting both the freight and the company's interests."

Effective daily communication with dispatchers represents one of the most valuable skills a professional driver can develop. It transforms the driver from simple freight mover to strategic partner in logistics operations, resulting in better assignments, improved working relationships, y enhanced earning potential throughout your career.

5.2 Escalación de Problemas y Toma de Decisiones

La escalación efectiva de problemas representa una de las habilidades más críticas en la comunicación conductor-despachador, donde la capacidad de transmitir información compleja y solicitar guidance apropiado puede determinar la diferencia entre una crisis well-managed y un disaster operacional costoso. Los despachadores dependen de conductores profesionales para provide situational awareness accurate y recommend solutions basadas en experiencia en carretera, mientras que los conductores necesitan support administrativo y authority para make decisions que exceden su direct control.

Navegando Weather Delays y Road Closures con Comunicación Estratégica

Weather-related delays presentan algunos de los challenges más complejos en transportation porque involucran safety considerations, regulatory compliance, customer expectations, y financial implications que deben balanced cuidadosamente through effective communication.

Cuando weather conditions comienzan a deteriorate, la comunicación proactive permite better decision-making para todas las parties involved: "I'm monitoring weather conditions on my planned route through Colorado, y forecast shows significant snow development over the next 12 hours. Current road conditions are manageable, pero DOT is forecasting possible chain requirements o complete closure on I-70 through the mountains. Should I accelerate my schedule para get through before conditions worsen, o should I plan para delay y wait para improvement?"

Esta comunicación demonstrates situational awareness, provides specific information about timing y potential impacts, y offers alternative strategies para dispatcher consideration. Es significantly más useful than simply saying "weather looks bad" porque provides actionable intelligence.

Para active weather emergencies, communication must be immediate y comprehensive: "I'm currently experiencing whiteout conditions on I-80 westbound en Wyoming near mile marker 215. Visibility es less than 50 feet, y multiple vehicles have slid off the roadway. I've safely exited at the nearest rest area y will wait for conditions para improve. This delay will impact my delivery schedule by at least 4-6 hours, y potentially longer if the storm continues as forecasted."

Road closures require detailed communication about alternatives y timing implications: "I-40 eastbound es completely closed due para accident cleanup between mile markers 180 y 195 con no estimated reopening time. The detour adds approximately 75 miles y 2.5 hours para my route. Combined con my current HOS status, this will push my delivery beyond the scheduled appointment time. Should I contact the customer directly about the delay, o would you prefer para handle rescheduling?"

Solicitando Guidance sobre Customer Issues y Delivery Problems

Customer-related problems often require escalation porque they involve contractual obligations, liability concerns, y relationship management que exceed the direct authority de individual drivers. Effective communication about these situations protects both driver y company interests while maintaining professional relationships.

Cuando receivers refuse freight for questionable reasons, communication should document the situation comprehensively: "The receiving clerk at [location] es refusing delivery, claiming the freight was scheduled para yesterday. However, my paperwork clearly shows today's date, y I have documentation showing I'm arriving within the scheduled window. The clerk es insisting they can't receive today y wants me para reschedule para next week. This seems like a customer scheduling error rather than a carrier problem, y I need guidance on how para proceed."

Para situations involving damaged freight discovered at delivery, communication must protect liability mientras maintaining customer relationships: "During unloading at [location], the receiver has identified damage para [specific items]. The damage appears para be [description] y affects approximately [quantity]. I need para determine whether this damage was pre-existing, occurred during transit, o happened during unloading. Should I document this as a joint inspection con the receiver, o do you want me para follow specific procedures para this customer?"

Access problems at delivery locations require immediate escalation cuando they affect safety o compliance: "I've arrived at the delivery location, pero the access road es impassable due para [specific condition]. The customer es requesting that I attempt delivery anyway, but I believe this would create unsafe conditions para both my vehicle y other traffic. I need authorization para either refuse the delivery attempt o request that the customer provide safe access before proceeding."

Negotiating Detention Time y Additional Compensation

Detention time negotiations require sophisticated communication que balances assertiveness con professionalism, protecting driver earnings mientras maintaining positive customer relationships que benefit long-term business operations.

Cuando detention time becomes apparent, early communication establishes expectations: "I've been at the [pickup/delivery] location para [time period] beyond the scheduled appointment, y it appears there will be additional delay due para [specific reason]. Based on our contract terms, I believe detention time should begin accruing at [time]. Should I document this delay officially, o are there other arrangements I should be aware of?"

Para extended delays que affect HOS compliance, communication must address both compensation y regulatory implications: "I've been waiting at this location para 4 hours beyond the scheduled time, which es affecting my available drive time para the remainder of today's schedule. If this delay continues much longer, I'll need para adjust my break timing para remain compliant con HOS regulations. This could impact delivery timing para subsequent loads unless we can arrange appropriate compensation para the extended detention."

Additional stop charges require clear communication about services provided: "The customer es requesting an additional stop that wasn't included en the original dispatch. The extra stop adds approximately [distance/time] para the route y requires [specific services]. Based on our standard rates, this should qualify para additional compensation of [amount]. Should I proceed con the extra stop con the understanding that appropriate charges will be applied?"

Expressing Safety Concerns y Unrealistic Timeline Pressures

Safety-related escalations represent the most critical communications porque they involve potential liability, regulatory compliance, y life-threatening situations que require immediate attention y support from dispatch management.

Cuando load assignments present safety concerns, communication must be direct y specific: "I have serious concerns about the safety of this load assignment. The delivery location requires access through [specific road/bridge] con weight restrictions of [limit], pero my gross weight es [actual weight]. Attempting this delivery would violate weight restrictions y potentially create dangerous conditions. I need alternative routing o arrangements before I can safely complete this delivery."

Para unrealistic timeline pressures que would require HOS violations, communication should reference specific regulations: "The timeline para this load assignment would require me para drive [hours] today, which exceeds my available drive time under current HOS regulations. To complete this assignment legally, I would need para [specific adjustment]. I want para ensure we maintain full compliance mientras meeting customer expectations."

Equipment safety issues require immediate escalation: "I've identified a safety issue con [specific equipment] that makes continued operation unsafe. The problem es [specific description] y poses risks para [specific safety concerns]. I've removed the vehicle from service y need immediate guidance about repair arrangements y alternative equipment para complete current assignments."

Cuando customer demands conflict con safety regulations, escalation protects both driver y company: "The customer at [location] es demanding that I [specific unsafe request] para expedite their delivery. This request violates [specific safety regulation o company policy] y could create liability issues. I need management support para maintain safe practices mientras explaining para the customer why their request cannot be accommodated."

Capítulo 6: Servicio al Cliente e Inglés de Entrega

Las habilidades profesionales de comunicación en inglés pueden aumentar las propinas y bonos de un camionero en un promedio de $3,000 por año. Esta cifra representa mucho más que dinero extra en el bolsillo; refleja el valor económico directo de la comunicación profesional en una industria donde las relaciones personales frecuentemente determinan oportunidades futuras, preferencias de carga, y recomendaciones que pueden transformar una carrera.

En el mundo del transporte comercial, cada entrega es una oportunidad de construir o dañar la reputación que te seguirá durante toda tu carrera. Los clientes que reciben entregas no solo evalúan la puntualidad y condición de su mercancía; también forman impresiones duraderas sobre la profesionalidad del conductor, la confiabilidad de la compañía transportista, y la calidad general del servicio que determina decisiones futuras de contratación.

Los consumidores y businesses modernos tienen expectativas cada vez más altas sobre servicio al cliente, influenciadas por empresas como Amazon que han establecido nuevos estándares para convenience, communication, y profesionalismo. Los conductores que pueden meeting estas expectativas mediante comunicación efectiva en inglés no solo proporcionan mejor servicio; también se posicionan como assets valiosos que contribuyen directamente al crecimiento y success de sus employers.

Este capítulo te equipará con las habilidades de comunicación específicas necesarias para excel en interacciones de customer service, transformando cada delivery en una opportunity para demonstrate professionalism que results en better relationships, improved earnings, y enhanced career prospects.

6.1 Interacciones Profesionales de Entrega

El Arte de las Primeras Impresiones en Deliveries

La primera impresión que creates cuando arrives at a delivery location sets the tone para toda la interaction y frecuentemente determines whether the experience será remembered positively o negatively. Professional drivers entienden que they represent not only themselves sino también their company, their industry, y the broader community de transportation professionals.

Effective arrival communication comienza before you exit your vehicle. Observing the delivery environment, understanding any posted signs o restrictions, y assessing the appropriate level de formality para la situation demonstrates situational awareness que customers appreciate. A construction site delivery requires different communication approach than a corporate office, pero both demand equal professionalism adapted para their specific contexts.

Saludos Profesionales y Establishment of Rapport

Professional greetings en delivery situations should balance friendliness con efficiency, acknowledging que customers have their own schedules y responsibilities while demonstrating that you value the business relationship.

Cuando approach a customer para delivery confirmation, your initial greeting should establish your identity y purpose clearly: "Good morning, I'm [your name] from [company name], y I have a delivery scheduled para [customer name o address]. Could you help me verify that I'm at the correct location y that you're ready para receive this shipment?"

Esta approach immediately provides all necessary identification information while confirming that you're at the right place y that timing es appropriate para the delivery. Es significantly more professional than simply asking "where do you want this stuff?" o assuming that your arrival será automatically expected.

Para deliveries at businesses where you may not know who has authority para receive shipments: "Excuse me, I have a freight delivery para this location. Could you direct me para whoever handles receiving? I want para make sure I follow your procedures correctly y get the shipment para the right department."

Esta communication demonstrates respect para the customer's internal processes while ensuring that you connect con the appropriate person who can efficiently handle the delivery. Es also shows proactive concern about following proper procedures rather than simply unloading wherever convenient.

Adapting Communication Style para Different Customer Types

Different types de customers require different communication approaches, pero all deserve the same level de professional respect y attention.

Para residential deliveries, communication often needs para be more explanatory: "I have a delivery para this address. The shipment contains [general description] from [sender]. I'll need someone para verify the delivery address y sign para receipt. Would you like me para place it en a specific location, o would you prefer para inspect it before I unload?"

Commercial deliveries typically involve more structured processes: "I'm here con the scheduled delivery para [specific department o contact]. I have [quantity y type] pieces con BOL number [number]. Who should I coordinate con para unloading, y are there any specific procedures I should follow para this location?"

High-security locations require additional documentation awareness: "I understand this es a secure facility. I have delivery authorization [number o contact name] y all required documentation. What es your procedure para vehicle inspection y escort durante unloading?"

Confirming Delivery Details y Managing Expectations

Thorough confirmation de delivery details protects both you y the customer from misunderstandings que could result en rejected deliveries, damaged relationships, o liability issues.

Delivery confirmation should include verification de key details: "Before we begin unloading, I'd like para confirm the delivery details. According para my documentation, you should be receiving [specific items], total quantity [number], delivered para [specific location o department]. Does this match your expectations?"

Para deliveries que involve specific timing requirements: "I know you requested delivery between [time range]. I'm here within that window, y the unloading should take approximately [time estimate]. Will this timing work con your schedule, o are there any constraints I should be aware of?"

Cuando deliveries involve special handling requirements: "My instructions indicate that this freight requires [specific handling]. I have the appropriate equipment y procedures para manage this safely. Is there anything specific about your receiving area that I should know before we start?"

Managing Customer Expectations About Delivery Processes

Customer education about delivery processes helps prevent frustration y ensures smoother operations while demonstrating your professional expertise.

Para customers unfamiliar con commercial deliveries: "I'll walk you through our delivery process so you know what para expect. First, I'll need para verify that you're authorized para receive this shipment. Then we'll confirm the contents together before unloading. Finally, you'll sign para receipt, y I'll provide you con a copy de all documentation."

Cuando explaining timing considerations: "The unloading process will take approximately [time] depending on [factors]. I want para make sure we have adequate time para handle everything safely y properly. If you have time constraints, please let me know so we can plan accordingly."

Para deliveries que require customer participation: "This delivery will require some coordination on your part. You'll need para [specific requirements] while I handle [specific responsibilities]. Working together, we can complete this efficiently y safely."

Explicando Procedimientos de Entrega y Requirements

Clear explanation de delivery procedures protects both parties y ensures that all regulatory y contractual requirements are met properly.

Signature requirements need clear explanation: "I'll need an authorized signature para confirm delivery. The person signing should be authorized para receive freight para your company y should verify that the shipment appears complete y undamaged before signing. Once you sign, you're accepting responsibility para the freight."

Para deliveries que involve inspection requirements: "Before you sign para receipt, you have the right para inspect the shipment para any visible damage. If you notice anything concerning, we should document it on the delivery receipt before completing the delivery. This protects both your interests y mine."

Cuando special documentation es required: "This delivery requires additional documentation beyond the standard delivery receipt. I need para get [specific information] y have you sign [specific forms]. This es required by [regulation o customer requirement] y ensures that we maintain proper records."

Handling Payment Requirements y Financial Transactions

Deliveries que involve payment collection require careful attention para procedures y documentation para protect all parties involved.

Para COD deliveries, explanation should be comprehensive: "This delivery requires payment on delivery en the amount de [amount]. I can accept [acceptable payment methods], y I'll provide you con a receipt para your payment along con proof de delivery. Do you have the payment ready, o do you need time para arrange it?"

Cuando payment discrepancies arise: "There appears para be a discrepancy between the amount due according para my documentation y what you were expecting. Let me double-check my paperwork, y perhaps you could verify your records so we can resolve this accurately."

Para situations involving additional charges: "My documentation shows additional charges de [amount] para [specific services]. These charges were added because [explanation]. If you have questions about these charges, I can provide the documentation, o you can contact our office directly."

Managing Special Requests y Last-Minute Changes

Special requests y changes require careful evaluation para determine what can be accommodated safely y legally while maintaining positive customer relationships.

Cuando customers request delivery modifications: "I understand you'd like para change [specific aspect] de the delivery. Let me check whether this change es something I can accommodate while maintaining safety y following company procedures. If I can't make this change, I'll explain why y see if there are alternatives que would work para you."

Para requests que exceed normal service: "I appreciate that you have special needs para this delivery, y I want para help if possible. However, [specific request] goes beyond our standard service capabilities. Let me contact my dispatcher para see if we can arrange something special, o if there are alternatives que would meet your needs."

Timing change requests require careful consideration: "You're asking para adjust the delivery timing from what was originally scheduled. I need para check my schedule y regulatory requirements para see if this change es possible. If I can accommodate it, I will, pero I also need para ensure I remain compliant con all transportation regulations."

Addressing Delivery Problems y Disputes Professionally

Cuando delivery problems arise, professional communication can often resolve issues satisfactorily para all parties while protecting business relationships.

Para damaged freight discovered durante delivery: "I notice some apparent damage para [specific items]. This could have occurred durante shipping, handling, o it might have been pre-existing. Let's document this condition together so que we have accurate records. You can still accept the delivery, pero the damage should be noted on the delivery receipt para insurance purposes."

Cuando quantity discrepancies are discovered: "There appears para be a difference between what my paperwork shows y what we're actually unloading. According para my bill de lading, there should be [quantity], pero I count [actual quantity]. Let's double-check this together y document the actual count para the delivery receipt."

Para deliveries que don't meet customer expectations: "I understand this delivery doesn't match what you were expecting. Let me review my documentation con you so we can understand where the discrepancy occurred. If there's been an error, we'll need para document it y determine the best way para resolve the situation."

Professional delivery interactions represent opportunities para differentiate yourself en a competitive industry mientras building the relationships que sustain long-term career success. Every positive customer interaction contributes para a reputation que opens doors para better opportunities, higher compensation, y increased job satisfaction throughout your transportation career.

6.2 Manejar Situaciones Difíciles

La gestión efectiva de situaciones problemáticas durante entregas representa una de las habilidades más valiosas que un conductor profesional puede desarrollar, donde la capacidad de transformar conflictos potenciales en resoluciones satisfactorias puede determinar la diferencia entre clientes perdidos y relaciones comerciales fortalecidas. Los problemas de entrega son inevitables en operaciones de transporte complejas, pero la manera en que estos problemas se manejan frecuentemente tiene más impacto en la relación comercial a largo plazo que el problema original.

Desescalando Conflictos sobre Mercancías Dañadas

Los descubrimientos de mercancía dañada durante la entrega crean situaciones emocionales cargadas donde los clientes pueden sentir frustración, pérdida financiera, y preocupación sobre interrupciones en sus operaciones. Tu respuesta inicial a estas situaciones establece si el problema se resolverá cooperativamente o se escalará hacia conflicto destructivo.

Cuando el daño se descubre durante la entrega, la comunicación inmediata debe combinar empatía con procedimientos apropiados: "I can see that you're concerned about the condition of this freight, and I completely understand your frustration. Let's work together to document exactly what we're seeing so that we can get this resolved properly for you. My first priority is making sure you get the resolution you deserve."

Esta aproximación reconoce las emociones del cliente mientras estableciendo un framework cooperativo para resolution. Es importante evitar language defensivo o attempts para minimizar concerns, which can escalate tensions unnecessarily.

Para situaciones donde el damage appears extensive o will significantly impact customer operations: "I realize this damage is going to create serious problems for your business, and I want to help get this resolved as quickly as possible. Let me document everything thoroughly and get my dispatch team involved immediately so we can start working on solutions. What's your most urgent concern that we need to address first?"

La documentation process debe involve customer participation: "I'd like you to help me document this damage so that we have accurate records from both perspectives. Could you describe what you're seeing from your standpoint while I record the details? This will help ensure that the insurance claim accurately reflects your experience."

Cuando customers become emotional about damaged freight, acknowledgment of their perspective es crucial: "I can understand why you're upset about this situation. This clearly isn't what you were expecting, and it's going to create problems for you. While I can't undo the damage, I can make sure we handle the documentation and follow-up properly so you get the best possible resolution."

Gestionando Entregas Tardías y Expectativas de Timing

Late deliveries create customer frustration que stems not only from inconvenience pero también from potential financial impacts, disrupted schedules, y broken commitments to their own customers. Effective communication about delays requires transparency, accountability, y proactive solution-seeking.

Para deliveries que arrive later than promised, immediate acknowledgment of the delay demonstrates respect para customer time: "I know I'm arriving later than the scheduled time, and I apologize for any inconvenience this has caused you. I want to explain what happened and work with you to minimize any impact on your operations."

Explanation of delay causes should be factual without over-explaining o making excuses: "The delay was caused by [specific reason], which was beyond our control. While this doesn't fix the inconvenience you've experienced, I wanted you to understand that this wasn't due to poor planning or lack of attention to your delivery."

Para customers whose operations have been affected by late deliveries: "I understand that my late arrival may have disrupted your schedule, and I'm concerned about how this affects your business. Is there anything I can do to help minimize the impact? Perhaps we can expedite the unloading process or coordinate with your team in a way that helps get you back on schedule."

Cuando late deliveries are part of a pattern rather than isolated incidents, honesty about broader issues while commitment to improvement es important: "I know this isn't the first time we've had timing issues with deliveries to your location, and I understand your frustration. This is something our company is actively working to improve, and I'll make sure your concerns about reliability are communicated to management."

Explicando Limitaciones del Transportista Profesionalmente

Transportation operations involve numerous factors outside direct driver control, including weather, traffic, customer delays, mechanical issues, y regulatory requirements. Explaining these limitations professionally helps customers understand the complexity of transportation while maintaining accountability para controllable factors.

Para situations involving regulatory limitations: "I'd like to help you with that request, but federal transportation regulations specifically prohibit [specific action]. These regulations are in place for safety reasons, and violating them would put both of us at risk legally. Let me see if there's an alternative way we can meet your needs within regulatory requirements."

Cuando equipment limitations prevent customer accommodation: "I understand you're hoping for [specific request], but my equipment isn't designed for that type of operation. Using the equipment incorrectly could damage both the freight and the equipment, which would create bigger problems for everyone. Are there alternative approaches that would work with the equipment I have?"

For timing limitations imposed by Hours of Service regulations: "I'd be happy to wait longer if it would help your operations, but federal hours-of-service regulations require me to [specific requirement] by [specific time]. If I don't comply with these regulations, it creates serious legal problems for both me and my company. Let's see if we can work within these constraints to find a solution."

Insurance y liability limitations require careful explanation: "I understand your concern about [specific issue], but our insurance coverage y liability agreements have specific limitations. This doesn't mean we don't care about your concerns; it means we need to handle this through the proper channels to ensure you get appropriate resolution."

Redirigiendo Quejas a Canales Apropiados

Effective complaint redirection maintains customer relationships while ensuring that issues reach people with authority y resources to provide meaningful resolution. The key es making redirection feel like helpful guidance rather than avoidance de responsibility.

Para issues beyond driver authority: "This is definitely something that needs attention, pero it's beyond what I can resolve directly. Let me give you the contact information for [specific person/department] who has the authority to handle this type of situation. I'll also make sure they know to expect your call y understand the urgency of your concerns."

Cuando complaints involve company policies o procedures: "I understand your frustration with [specific policy], pero policy decisions are made at a management level where I don't have input. However, I can tell you exactly who you should speak with to discuss this, y I'll document your concerns in my delivery report so they're aware of the issue."

Para billing o contract disputes: "Financial issues like this need to be handled by our accounting department, who have access to all the contract details y billing information. I can give you their direct contact information, y I'll note in my report that you have concerns about billing so they can prioritize your inquiry."

Redirection should include follow-up commitment: "I'm going to personally follow up on this issue to make sure it gets proper attention. While I can't resolve it directly, I can ensure that the right people know about your concerns y that you get the response you deserve."

Capítulo 7: Cumplimiento Regulatorio y Comunicación DOT

Las violaciones DOT debido a barreras de comunicación resultan en un promedio de $8,500 en multas por incidente para conductores comerciales. Esta cifra representa mucho más que simplemente el costo financiero directo; incluye tiempo perdido fuera de servicio, impacto en CSA scores que afectan oportunidades futuras de empleo, y el stress de navegar procesos legales complejos que pueden extenderse durante meses. Para conductores que operan en territorio de habla inglesa, la incapacidad de comunicarse efectivamente durante inspecciones DOT puede transformar violaciones menores en problemas mayores, y situaciones de rutina en pesadillas burocráticas.

Los inspectores del Departamento de Transporte operan bajo protocolos estrictos diseñados para asegurar uniformity y fairness en enforcement, pero también tienen considerable discreción en cómo interpretan situaciones y aplican regulaciones. La comunicación efectiva puede influenciar significativamente el outcome de inspecciones, no through manipulation o deception, sino through clear presentation de facts, demonstration de professionalism, y cooperation que facilita thorough pero efficient inspections.

Modern DOT enforcement ha evolucionado from simple safety checks hacia comprehensive evaluations que examine not only vehicle condition sino también driver qualifications, hours-of-service compliance, cargo securement, hazmat procedures, y dozens de otros regulatory requirements. Cada uno de estos areas requires specific vocabulary, understanding de regulatory frameworks, y communication skills que demonstrate competence y cooperation con enforcement officers.

La comunicación profesional durante DOT interactions no es about avoiding legitimate enforcement; es about ensuring que inspections proceed smoothly, que all relevant information es communicated accurately, y que any violations identified are addressed appropriately. Professional drivers who master these communication skills find que inspections become less stressful, more predictable, y significantly less likely to result en misunderstandings que could lead para unnecessary penalties.

7.1 Comunicación en Inspecciones en Carretera

Understanding the Hierarchy y Scope de DOT Inspection Levels

DOT inspections operate under a structured system de six different levels, cada uno con specific scope, procedures, y communication requirements que drivers must understand para respond appropriately y ensure thorough compliance verification.

Level I inspections represent the most comprehensive examination de both driver y vehicle, requiring extensive documentation y systematic verification de multiple regulatory compliance areas. Cuando an inspector indicates que a Level I inspection will be conducted, your initial response should demonstrate understanding de the process y cooperation: "I understand this will be a complete inspection. I have all my documentation ready, including my medical certificate, logbook, vehicle registration, y any permits or special authorizations. Would you like me to organize these documents en a specific order para make your inspection more efficient?"

Esta communication approach demonstrates several important elements: recognition de the inspection scope, preparedness con required documentation, y willingness para facilitate the inspector's work. These factors contribute para positive inspector relationships que can result en more efficient inspections y professional treatment throughout the process.

Level II inspections focus primarily on driver qualifications y administrative compliance, requiring different preparation y communication focus: "I understand you'll be conducting a driver qualification inspection. I have my CDL, medical certificate, logbook, y any endorsement documentation readily available. Are there specific aspects de my qualifications que you'd like para review first?"

Level III inspections concentrate on driver-only requirements without vehicle examination, typically occurring at weigh stations o during traffic stops: "I have all my driver qualification documents con me. My logbook is current y accurate, y I'm operating within all hours-of-service requirements. What specific documentation would you like para see first?"

The comunicación approach para each inspection level should reflect understanding de what inspectors will examine y demonstrate que you maintain appropriate documentation y compliance awareness para that specific scope de inspection.

Responding para Inspector Questions y Requests Professionally

Inspector interactions require careful balance between cooperation y self-protection, providing requested information accurately while avoiding unnecessary elaboration que could create problems o misunderstandings.

Cuando inspectors request documentation, your response should be immediate y organized: "Here's my logbook, current as de this morning. You'll see that I completed my last 10-hour break at [location] ending at [time], y I have [hours] remaining on my drive clock today. All entries are accurate y complete according para federal requirements."

Esta type de response provides specific information efficiently while demonstrating knowledge de regulatory requirements y attention para detail in record-keeping. Es significantly more professional than simply handing over documents without explanation o context.

Para questions about vehicle condition o pre-trip inspections: "I completed a thorough pre-trip inspection this morning before beginning operations. I identified [any defects found] y have documentation showing [how defects were addressed]. The vehicle inspection report es current y shows no defects que would affect safe operation."

Cuando inspectors discover potential violations, your communication should be factual y non-defensive: "I see what you're pointing out, y I want para understand the specific regulation que applies here. Could you help me understand what needs para be corrected para bring this into compliance? I'm committed para operating safely y legally."

Este approach acknowledges the inspector's findings without admitting fault, requests clarification about specific requirements, y demonstrates commitment para compliance. Es important para avoid argumentative o defensive responses que could escalate tensions unnecessarily.

Explaining Special Permits y Operating Authorities

Special permits y operating authorities require specific communication because they often involve exceptions para standard regulations que inspectors may not encounter frequently. Your explanation should be clear, supported by proper documentation, y demonstrate understanding de the permit conditions.

Para oversize o overweight permits: "I'm operating under permit number [number] issued by [authority] para this specific load. The permit authorizes operation at [specific weight/dimensions] y includes routing restrictions que I'm following exactly. Here's the permit documentation, y you can see that I'm within all specified limitations."

Hazmat authorizations require particularly detailed explanation: "I hold a current hazmat endorsement y am transporting [specific material] under proper classification [UN number]. The material es properly placarded, documented, y secured according para federal regulations. I have all required shipping papers, emergency response information, y security plan documentation."

Interstate operating authority communications should reference specific regulatory frameworks: "I'm operating under [type de authority] issued by FMCSA. My operations are limited para [specific scope], y this load falls within my authorized operating parameters. I have current registration y insurance documentation that meets federal requirements."

Cuando permits have specific timing o routing requirements: "This permit requires me para follow [specific route] y complete transit by [specific time]. I'm currently ahead de schedule y following the designated route exactly. The permit includes specific rest area designations que I'm using para required breaks."

Managing Agricultural Exemptions y Seasonal Regulations

Agricultural operations often involve complex exemptions y seasonal regulations que require sophisticated communication because they frequently modify standard DOT requirements en ways que inspectors may not immediately recognize.

Inglés para camioneros

Para harvest season exemptions: "I'm operating under agricultural exemption provisions defined en 49 CFR 395.1(k) during harvest season para [specific crop]. This exemption allows [specific modifications para standard requirements] within [geographic limitations]. I have documentation from [authority] confirming que current conditions qualify para this exemption."

Agricultural commodity hauling exemptions require specific regulatory knowledge: "I'm transporting agricultural commodities within the [distance] mile exemption radius from the source. This qualifies para exemption from [specific regulations] under federal agricultural provisions. The commodity originated at [location] y es being delivered within the exempted zone."

Seasonal weight exemptions need careful explanation: "During harvest season, this state allows increased weight limits para agricultural commodities. I'm operating under permit [number] que authorizes operation at [weight] during the period from [date] through [date]. My current load weighs [actual weight] y es within permitted limits."

Para equipment exemptions related para agricultural operations: "This vehicle configuration es specifically authorized para agricultural use under [regulation]. While it may appear para exceed standard limitations, agricultural exemptions allow [specific modifications] when transporting [specific commodities] during [specific timeframes]."

Communicating About Vehicle Modifications y Equipment Variations

Modern commercial vehicles often include modifications o specialized equipment que may not be immediately familiar para all inspectors, requiring clear explanation para prevent misunderstandings about compliance.

Para emission control modifications: "This vehicle has been modified con [specific equipment] para meet [specific emission requirements]. The modifications were performed by [certified installer] y are documented here. The equipment remains compliant con all federal y state emission regulations."

Specialized securement equipment may require explanation: "The load securement system on this trailer es designed specifically para [type de cargo]. While it may look different from standard systems, it meets o exceeds all DOT securement requirements para this type de freight. Here's the manufacturer documentation showing compliance."

Electronic system modifications should be explained clearly: "This vehicle es equipped con [specific electronic systems] que may interface con standard DOT requirements differently. The systems are compliant con all federal regulations y provide [specific benefits]. I have certification documentation showing proper installation y calibration."

Safety equipment variations require detailed explanation: "This vehicle carries additional safety equipment beyond minimum requirements because de [specific operational needs]. The equipment includes [specific items] y es maintained according para [specific standards]. This represents enhanced safety compliance rather than deviation from requirements."

Managing Documentation Discrepancies y Regulatory Questions

Even well-prepared drivers occasionally encounter documentation discrepancies o regulatory questions que require careful communication para resolve without creating unnecessary complications.

Para minor documentation errors: "I notice there's an error en [specific document]. The error es [specific description] y should read [correct information]. I have supporting documentation que shows the correct information, y I'll make sure this es corrected properly para future compliance."

Cuando regulations seem para conflict: "I'm encountering what appears para be conflicting requirements between [regulation A] y [regulation B]. Could you help me understand how these regulations work together en this specific situation? I want para ensure I'm complying con all applicable requirements."

Para questions about recent regulatory changes: "I want para make sure I'm operating under current regulations. I've been following [specific procedure] based on my understanding de current requirements. If there have been recent changes que affect this, could you help me understand what adjustments I need para make?"

Documentation timing issues require careful explanation: "This document shows [date] which may appear para be [issue]. However, the timing es correct because [explanation de timing requirements]. I have additional documentation que clarifies the proper timeline para this requirement."

Professional Response para Violations y Citations

Cuando violations are identified during inspections, professional communication can influence how situations are resolved y may affect the severity de penalties imposed.

Para violations que are immediately correctable: "I understand the violation y can correct it immediately. What specific action do you need me para take para bring this into compliance? I'm prepared para make the correction now y document it properly."

Cuando violations require out-of-service time: "I understand that this violation requires me para go out de service until corrected. Could you help me understand the specific requirements para getting back en service? I want para make sure I complete all necessary steps properly."

Para paperwork violations que can be resolved through documentation: "I believe I have additional documentation que addresses this issue. Would you like me para locate y present that information? I maintain comprehensive records y may have supporting documents que clarify the situation."

Cuando requesting reconsideration de inspection results: "I respect your professional judgment, pero I believe there may be a misunderstanding about [specific issue]. Could we review [specific documentation o regulation] together? I'm not trying para avoid responsibility, pero I want para ensure accurate application de regulations."

Professional communication during DOT inspections represents one de the most critical skills para commercial drivers, directly affecting legal compliance, financial outcomes, y career longevity. Mastering these communication techniques transforms potentially stressful encounters into professional interactions que demonstrate competence y cooperation mientras protecting your interests y rights under transportation law.

7.2 Discusiones sobre Horas de Servicio y ELD

Las regulaciones de horas de servicio representan uno de los aspectos más complejos y estrictamente monitoreados del cumplimiento DOT, donde la comunicación precisa puede ser la diferencia entre una inspección de rutina y violaciones costosas que afectan tu CSA score y elegibilidad para empleo futuro. Los Electronic Logging Devices han transformado fundamentalmente cómo se documenta y verifica el cumplimiento de HOS, creando nuevas oportunidades para precision pero también nuevos challenges para communication cuando surgen discrepancies o equipment failures.

Explicando Sleeper Berth Provisions y Strategic Rest Planning

Las sleeper berth provisions proporcionan flexibility crucial para operations de long-haul, pero require sophisticated understanding para communication effective con inspectors que pueden no estar familiarizados con todas las nuances de these regulations.

Cuando utilizes split sleeper berth operations, la explanation debe ser comprehensive y supported por clear documentation: "I'm using the split sleeper berth provision under 49 CFR 395.1(g). I took my first rest period of [duration] hours starting at [time] at [location]. This rest period, combined con my current sleeper berth time, allows me para extend my 14-hour window while maintaining required rest. My ELD shows both rest periods y the calculation of available drive time."

La communication about complex sleeper berth scenarios requires step-by-step explanation: "I understand this may look complicated on the logs, pero here's how the split sleeper provision works en my specific situation. My first qualifying rest period was [details], which paused my 14-hour clock. My current sleeper time, combined con the previous rest, provides me con [available hours] under the split sleeper calculation."

Para situations donde sleeper berth time es interrupted by other activities: "During my sleeper berth time, I briefly moved the vehicle para [reason] without going on duty. This movement es permitted under sleeper berth regulations as long as the rest period continues uninterrupted. The ELD correctly shows continuous sleeper berth time except para the brief movement."

Managing 34-Hour Restart Communications

The 34-hour restart provision offers important strategic options para drivers, pero requires careful documentation y communication para ensure compliance con all requirements including the weekly limitations.

Cuando planning o explaining restart calculations: "I'm taking a 34-hour restart beginning at [time] on [date]. This restart will reset my 60/70-hour clock y allow me para begin con full hours available. According para my logs, this es my [first/second] restart this week, which complies con the weekly restart limitations."

Para complex restart scenarios involving multiple time zones o irregular schedules: "I began this restart at [time] en [time zone], y it will complete at [time] en [time zone]. The restart spans two consecutive periods including [specific time periods] as required by regulation. My ELD calculates the restart automatically, pero I wanted para explain the timing para clarity."

Cuando restart timing affects operational schedules: "My 34-hour restart will complete at [time], which means I'll be available para duty at that time con full hours. This timing coordinates con my scheduled pickup at [time] y allows adequate time para the planned route while maintaining compliance."

Personal Conveyance Communications y Documentation

Personal conveyance regulations provide valuable flexibility pero require careful communication because they involve exceptions para normal on-duty requirements que may not be immediately obvious para enforcement officers.

Cuando using personal conveyance para parking: "I used personal conveyance para move from [location] para [location] para obtain required rest. This movement was necessary because adequate parking wasn't available at my delivery location, y the movement was solely para personal rest purposes, not business convenience."

Para personal conveyance combined con other activities: "The personal conveyance time shown on my ELD was para [specific personal purpose]. During this time, I didn't perform any work-related activities, y the movement was entirely para personal reasons. I have documentation supporting the personal nature of this travel."

Cuando personal conveyance timing may appear irregular: "I understand the personal conveyance entry may look unusual, pero it represents [specific personal need]. The movement wasn't related para business operations o load assignments, y I was completely off duty para personal purposes during this time."

ELD Malfunctions y Paper Log Procedures

ELD malfunctions create significant documentation challenges que require immediate attention y clear communication con enforcement officers who must verify compliance through alternative means.

Cuando reporting ELD malfunctions para inspectors: "My ELD experienced a malfunction starting at [time] on [date]. I immediately reverted para paper logs as required by regulation y have maintained accurate records since the malfunction occurred. I have documentation of attempts para repair the device y the technical support efforts that have been made."

Para explaining paper log accuracy durante ELD outages: "These paper logs reflect my actual duty status desde the ELD malfunction. I've been extremely careful para maintain accuracy, including [specific examples of documentation]. I have supporting documentation such as fuel receipts, delivery confirmations, y GPS records que verify the accuracy of these manual entries."

Cuando ELD repairs affect log continuity: "The ELD has been repaired y es now functioning properly. There's a gap en electronic records from [time] para [time] during the malfunction period, pero I have complete paper logs covering this entire period. The repair shop provided documentation confirming the nature of the malfunction y the repairs performed."

Para complex ELD diagnostic issues: "The ELD has been experiencing intermittent problems que haven't been resolved despite multiple repair attempts. I have documentation from [service provider] showing the ongoing diagnostic efforts. I've been maintaining backup paper logs para ensure continuous compliance documentation."

Team Driving Operations y Passenger Authorization

Team driving operations involve complex HOS interactions y passenger authorization requirements que require sophisticated communication para ensure complete understanding by enforcement officers.

Cuando explaining team driver operations: "This es a team operation con two qualified drivers. My co-driver es [name] con CDL [number]. We alternate driving duties according para HOS regulations, con the off-duty driver using sleeper berth time while the other driver operates the vehicle. Our logs show proper coordination para ensure continuous operation within legal limits."

Para team operations involving complex scheduling: "As a team operation, we coordinate our HOS para maximize efficiency while maintaining compliance. The current schedule shows [driver A] driving until [time], at which point [driver B] will take over. This allows continuous operation while both drivers maintain required rest periods."

Cuando team drivers share vehicles pero operate independently: "While we both drive this vehicle, we operate independently rather than as a coordinated team. Each driver maintains individual HOS compliance, y we coordinate vehicle use para ensure both drivers have access para their scheduled operations without interfering con each other's rest requirements."

Para passenger authorization en commercial vehicles: "I have authorization para carry [specific passenger] under [specific regulation/company policy]. The passenger es [relationship/authorization], y I have documentation showing proper authorization para this passenger para be en the commercial vehicle during operations."

Inglés para camioneros

Capítulo 8: Servicios de Gasolineras y Paradas de Camiones

La comunicación efectiva en paradas de combustible puede ahorrarle a los propietarios-operadores hasta $4,000 anuales a través de mejores programas de combustible y negociaciones de recompensas. Esta cifra no incluye los ahorros adicionales que resultan de resolver problemas rápidamente, evitar tiempo perdido en disputas de pago, y acceder a servicios de valor agregado que mejoran la eficiencia operacional. En una industria donde los márgenes de ganancia son ajustados y los costos de combustible representan frecuentemente el 25-30% de los gastos operacionales totales, cada dólar ahorrado en estaciones de servicio se traduce directamente en mayor rentabilidad.

Las paradas de camiones modernas han evolucionado desde simples estaciones de combustible hacia centros de servicios comprehensivos que ofrecen everything desde maintenance básico hasta dining, entertainment, y services logísticos. Para drivers profesionales, estas facilities representan más que simple refueling stops; son business hubs donde networking, information sharing, y strategic planning occur alongside routine vehicle services.

La communication efectiva en estos environments requiere understanding de complex pricing structures, reward programs, payment systems, y service offerings que pueden dramatically affect your operational costs y efficiency. Drivers who master these interactions position themselves para take advantage de competitive pricing, loyalty benefits, y value-added services que compound over time into significant economic advantages.

Las truck stops también serve como critical information exchanges donde drivers share road conditions, enforcement activity, customer experiences, y market intelligence que influences operational decisions. Professional communication skills en these environments contribute para building the networks y relationships que sustain successful long-term careers en transportation.

8.1 Negociaciones de Compra y Pago de Combustible

La Complejidad Oculta de Fuel Pricing y Program Management

Modern fuel purchasing para commercial vehicles involves sophisticated pricing structures que include base prices, taxes, fees, discounts, rebates, y loyalty programs que interact en ways que can significantly impact your bottom line. Understanding these systems y communicating effectively about them requires knowledge que goes far beyond simply pulling up para a pump y swiping a card.

Fuel pricing para commercial vehicles operates under different structures than retail automotive fueling, with wholesale pricing, fleet discounts, network benefits, y volume incentives que require strategic thinking y professional communication para maximize.

The difference between casual fuel purchasing y strategic fuel management can easily amount para thousands de dollars annually para active drivers.

Understanding Fuel Discount Programs y Network Benefits

Fuel discount programs operate under complex structures que reward loyalty, volume, y strategic purchasing behavior. Effective communication about these programs requires understanding tanto their benefits como their limitations, y being able para articulate your needs y expectations clearly para program representatives.

Cuando you're evaluating fuel discount programs, your communication should demonstrate understanding de your operational patterns: "I typically purchase between [gallons] y [gallons] per month, primarily along routes que cover [geographic areas]. I'm interested en understanding how your discount program works para drivers con my volume y routing patterns. Could you explain the discount structure y any additional benefits que might apply para my operation?"

Esta approach provides specific information que allows program representatives para offer tailored advice mientras demonstrating que you understand the factors que affect program benefits. Generic inquiries about "the best deal" rarely result en optimal program selection because they don't provide sufficient information para meaningful comparison.

Para existing program members seeking para optimize benefits: "I've been a member de your fuel program para [time period] y have purchased approximately [volume] during that time. I want para make sure I'm maximizing all available benefits. Are there additional services o purchasing strategies que could increase my discounts o provide other value?"

Cuando comparing multiple programs, communication should focus on total value rather than single metrics: "I'm comparing fuel programs y want para understand the total value proposition rather than just the per-gallon discount. What additional benefits does your program offer, such as maintenance discounts, priority services, o partner benefits que add value beyond fuel savings?"

Network coverage questions require specific geographic information: "My routes primarily cover [specific regions], y I need para ensure adequate network coverage para efficient trip planning. Could you show me network density en these areas y identify any gaps que might affect my ability para take advantage de program benefits?"

Managing Card Authorization Issues y Payment Disputes

Card authorization problems can create significant delays y frustration, particularly when they occur during tight scheduling windows o en remote locations where alternative payment options may be limited. Professional communication about these issues can expedite resolution y prevent recurring problems.

Cuando authorization issues occur, immediate communication should provide comprehensive information: "I'm experiencing a card authorization problem at pump [number]. My card number es [number], y the transaction amount es [amount]. The error message shows [specific message]. I've verified que my account es current y should have adequate credit available. Could you help me resolve this authorization issue?"

Esta communication provides all relevant technical information while indicating que you've already performed basic troubleshooting, which helps customer service representatives diagnose the problem efficiently.

Para recurring authorization problems: "I've been experiencing repeated authorization problems con card [number] over the past [time period]. The problems seem para occur [specific pattern], y I've confirmed que my account status es current. This es affecting my operational efficiency, y I need para identify y resolve the underlying cause."

Cuando authorization problems affect multiple locations o network-wide issues: "I've encountered authorization problems at multiple locations today, which suggests a network o system issue rather than a card-specific problem. Are you aware de any system problems que might be affecting card processing across your network?"

Payment disputes require careful documentation y clear communication: "I'm disputing a charge de [amount] from [date] at [location]. According para my records, the actual purchase was [amount], pero my statement shows [disputed amount]. I have [supporting documentation] que confirms the correct transaction amount."

DEF Requirements y Auxiliary Fluid Management

Diesel Exhaust Fluid has become a critical operational requirement para modern commercial vehicles, creating new purchasing, storage, y logistics considerations que require professional communication para manage effectively.

Cuando purchasing DEF en bulk quantities: "I need para purchase [quantity] gallons de DEF para my operation. I want para ensure I'm getting high-quality fluid que meets ISO 22241 standards. Do you have batch testing information available, y what's your storage y handling procedure para maintaining fluid quality?"

Esta communication demonstrates understanding de DEF quality requirements mientras seeking assurance que the supplier maintains appropriate quality controls. DEF contamination can cause expensive emission system problems, making quality verification important.

Para DEF storage y logistics questions: "I'm planning para store [quantity] de DEF para [time period]. Could you provide guidance about proper storage conditions para maintain fluid quality? I also need para understand shelf life y any special handling requirements para bulk storage."

Cuando DEF system problems affect purchasing decisions: "My vehicle es experiencing DEF system issues que may be related para fluid quality. I want para ensure que any DEF I purchase meets all specifications y won't contribute para system problems. Do you have quality documentation o testing results available para review?"

Para fleet operators managing multiple vehicles: "I'm managing DEF purchasing para [number] vehicles con varying consumption rates. I need para establish a purchasing strategy que ensures adequate supply while minimizing waste from aged fluid. Could you help me design a purchasing plan que optimizes both cost y quality?"

Reefer Fuel Management y Auxiliary Power Requirements

Refrigerated trailers create additional fuel management complexity que requires specialized communication about auxiliary fuel systems, consumption monitoring, y cost allocation between traction y refrigeration units.

Cuando comunicating about reefer fuel needs: "I'm operating a refrigerated trailer que requires [type] fuel para the refrigeration unit. The reefer consumes approximately [consumption rate] per hour, y I need para ensure adequate fuel supply para [duration] de operation. Do you have appropriate dispensing equipment para reefer fueling?"

Esta communication provides specific technical information about equipment requirements mientras indicating planning consciousness about fuel consumption y trip duration.

Para situations involving reefer fuel quality issues: "I'm experiencing problems con my refrigeration unit que may be related para fuel quality. The unit es [specific symptoms], y I suspect fuel contamination o quality issues. Do you have fuel quality testing available, o can you recommend steps para diagnosing fuel-related problems?"

Reefer fuel cost management requires separate tracking systems: "I need para purchase fuel para both my tractor y refrigerated trailer separately para cost accounting purposes. My company requires separate billing para traction fuel versus reefer fuel. Can your system accommodate split billing para these different fuel uses?"

Cuando coordinating reefer fuel con delivery schedules: "I have a temperature-sensitive load que requires continuous refrigeration para [duration]. I need para calculate total fuel requirements including both traction y reefer consumption para ensure adequate supply throughout the trip. Could you help me calculate total fuel needs based on [trip parameters]?"

Resolving Pump Problems y Equipment Issues

Pump malfunctions y equipment problems can create significant delays y require immediate attention para maintain operational schedules, particularly when alternatives aren't readily available.

Cuando reporting pump malfunctions: "Pump number [number] appears para be malfunctioning. The specific problem es [detailed description], y I've tried [troubleshooting steps]. The pump [specific behavior], y I need immediate assistance para either repair this pump o direct me para an alternative."

Esta communication provides specific technical information about the problem mientras indicating que you've attempted basic troubleshooting, which helps maintenance personnel diagnose y respond appropriately.

Para situations involving fuel quality concerns discovered durante pumping: "I noticed [specific observation] durante fueling at pump [number] que suggests possible fuel quality issues. The fuel [specific characteristics], which es unusual. I'm concerned about potential contamination o quality problems que could affect my engine."

Cuando equipment problems affect transaction completion: "I've completed fueling pero the pump won't finalize the transaction. The display shows [specific information], pero I can't get a receipt o complete the payment process. I need assistance para complete this transaction properly."

DEF equipment problems require specialized communication: "The DEF pump at bay [number] es not dispensing properly. The pump [specific behavior], y I'm unable para complete DEF filling para my vehicle. Since DEF es required para legal operation, I need immediate assistance para resolve this issue o access alternative DEF supplies."

Strategic Fuel Management y Cost Optimization

Professional fuel management involves strategic thinking about routing, timing, pricing, y program benefits que requires sophisticated communication con fuel suppliers y program administrators.

Cuando planning fuel purchases para optimize program benefits: "I'm planning a route que will require fuel purchases at [locations] over [timeframe]. I want para optimize my purchasing strategy para maximize program benefits y minimize total costs. Could you help me identify the best purchasing pattern para this trip?"

Para annual fuel planning discussions: "I'm developing my fuel purchasing strategy para next year based on anticipated mileage de [miles] y current consumption patterns. I want para evaluate different program options y purchasing strategies para optimize my total fuel costs. What information do you need para help me analyze program alternatives?"

Volume discount negotiations require professional presentation: "My operation purchases approximately [volume] gallons annually, y I'm interested en exploring volume discount opportunities. I can provide detailed purchasing history y projections para demonstrate volume consistency. What volume discount programs are available para operations de my size?"

Cuando seeking program modifications o special arrangements: "My operational patterns include [specific characteristics] que may not fit standard program structures. I'm interested en discussing whether program modifications o special arrangements might be available para better accommodate my unique operational needs."

Professional fuel purchasing communication demonstrates business acumen que can result en significant cost savings, improved service, y access para programs y benefits que compound over time into substantial competitive advantages para your transportation operation.

8.2 Servicios y Amenidades de Paradas de Camiones

Las paradas de camiones modernas han evolucionado hacia centros de servicios integrales que funcionan como hubs temporales para la vida de los conductores profesionales, ofreciendo amenidades que van desde necesidades básicas hasta servicios de lujo que pueden transformar significativamente la calidad de vida en carretera. La comunicación efectiva para acceder a estos servicios no solo mejora la experiencia inmediata, sino que también puede resultar en ahorros de tiempo y dinero, así como en el establecimiento de relaciones que faciliten servicios prioritarios y beneficios especiales.

Reservas de Estacionamiento y Gestión de Espacios

Inglés para camioneros

La gestión del estacionamiento en paradas de camiones representa uno de los challenges más significant para drivers profesionales, especialmente durante peak hours cuando la demand excede dramatically la available supply. Professional communication about parking needs puede mean la difference entre secure overnight parking y potentially dangerous roadside stops.

Cuando comuniques con truck stop management about parking availability, tu approach debe ser strategic y professional: "I'm planning to arrive at your location around [time] y will need parking para [duration]. Based on your typical traffic patterns, what's the likelihood de space availability at that time? If parking es likely para be full, are there overflow areas o alternative arrangements que you recommend?"

Esta communication demonstrates planning consciousness mientras seeking practical advice from staff who understand location-specific patterns. Es significantly more effective than simply arriving y hoping para space availability.

Para extended parking needs que exceed typical overnight stays: "I need extended parking para [duration] due para [legitimate reason such as mandatory rest, maintenance, o load scheduling]. What are your policies para extended stays, y are there additional fees o special arrangements required para parking beyond standard overnight periods?"

Cuando parking problems arise durante peak demand: "I understand que parking es full, pero I'm approaching my HOS limits y need para find safe parking soon. Are there alternative areas within your facility que might accommodate one more truck safely? I'm willing para pay additional fees para any available space que meets safety requirements."

Reservation systems, where available, require clear communication about specific needs: "I'd like para make a parking reservation para [date] arrival around [time]. I'm driving a [vehicle configuration] y will need space para [duration]. Do you have availability, y what information do you need para confirm this reservation?"

Shower Facilities y Personal Services Management

Shower facilities at truck stops represent critical amenities para professional drivers, particularly durante long-haul operations where access para personal hygiene facilities directly affects health, comfort, y professional appearance during customer interactions.

Cuando reserving shower facilities during busy periods: "I'd like para reserve a shower para [preferred time]. I understand there may be a wait durante peak hours. Could you give me an estimated wait time y put me on the list? I'm flexible con timing within [time range] if earlier slots become available."

Professional communication about shower facility quality concerns should be constructive: "I used shower number [number] y noticed [specific issue]. I wanted para bring this para your attention so it can be addressed. These facilities are important para professional drivers, y maintaining high standards helps differentiate your location from competitors."

Para shower packages que include additional amenities: "I'm interested en your premium shower package que includes [specific amenities]. Could you explain exactly what's included y help me understand the value comparison con standard shower facilities? I'm particularly interested en [specific amenity] for my operation."

Cuando shower facility problems affect planned schedule: "I have a customer meeting later today y need para maintain professional appearance. The shower I reserved has [specific problem]. What alternatives are available para ensure I can meet my professional obligations on schedule?"

Restaurant Services y Dietary Requirements

Truck stop restaurants serve diverse clientele con varying dietary needs, cultural preferences, y health requirements que require accommodating communication from both customers y staff. Professional drivers who can communicate effectively about food services often receive better attention y customized service que improves their dining experience.

Cuando communicating about specific dietary restrictions: "I have [specific dietary restriction] y need para ensure que my meal meets these requirements. Could you help me identify menu options que would be appropriate? I'm also concerned about cross-contamination, so I need para understand your kitchen procedures para handling special dietary needs."

Esta approach provides specific information about your needs mientras demonstrating understanding que accommodation may require special procedures. Es more effective than simply asking for "healthy options" o making vague requests about dietary preferences.

Para cultural o religious dietary requirements: "I follow [specific dietary guidelines] para religious reasons. Could you help me understand which menu items comply con these requirements? I'm particularly concerned about [specific ingredients o preparation methods] que would make items unsuitable para my dietary needs."

Cuando meal timing affects operational schedules: "I need para coordinate my meal con my driving schedule due para HOS requirements. I have approximately [time available] before I need para be back on duty. Could you recommend menu items que can be prepared quickly, o would it be possible para place an order para pickup at a specific time?"

Custom meal requests should be reasonable pero clearly communicated: "I know this isn't exactly on the menu, pero would it be possible para prepare [specific modification] para my dietary needs? I'm willing para pay additional charges para customization if necessary. I'm a regular customer y would appreciate any accommodation you can provide."

WiFi Access y Digital Services

Internet connectivity has become essential para modern truck operations, supporting everything from dispatch communication para personal entertainment durante mandatory rest periods. Professional communication about digital services ensures reliable access y helps troubleshoot problems que could affect operational efficiency.

Cuando seeking WiFi access information: "I need reliable internet access para both business communications y personal use durante my rest period. What WiFi options do you offer, y what's the performance level I can expect? I need sufficient bandwidth para [specific business applications] y want para understand any usage limitations."

Para extended internet usage needs: "I'll be parked here para [duration] y will need continuous internet access para business operations. Do you offer plans para extended use, y what's the cost structure? I'm particularly concerned about data limits que might affect my ability para maintain business communications."

Cuando experiencing connectivity problems: "I'm having trouble con the WiFi connection. I've tried [troubleshooting steps] pero still can't maintain reliable connectivity. Could you help me resolve this issue? I have business communications que are time-sensitive y need stable internet access."

Para business-critical internet needs: "I conduct business operations que require reliable, high-speed internet access. Do you have premium o business-class internet services available? I'm willing para pay additional fees para guaranteed performance levels que support my business requirements."

Lavandería y Maintenance de Personal Items

Laundry services represent important amenities para drivers on extended trips, where clean clothing directly affects professional appearance y personal comfort. Effective communication about these services ensures efficient use y optimal results.

Cuando using laundry facilities para the first time: "I'm not familiar con your laundry procedures. Could you explain how the machines work, what detergent options are available, y any special instructions para optimal results? I have [types de clothing] que may require different treatment."

Para time-sensitive laundry needs: "I have a customer appointment tomorrow y need para ensure my clothing es properly cleaned y dried by [specific time]. Based on machine cycle times, what's the latest I can start laundry para completion by my deadline? Are there expedited options available if needed?"

Specialty clothing care requires specific communication: "I have [type de clothing] que requires special care. Do your machines have appropriate settings para delicate items, o do you recommend hand washing? I want para avoid damage para professional clothing que es expensive para replace."

When laundry equipment problems occur: "Machine number [number] appears para have a problem. It [specific issue] y I'm concerned about potential damage para my clothing. Could you check the machine y either repair it o provide an alternative? I need para complete laundry para my schedule."

www.ingramcontent.com/pod-product-compliance
Lightning Source LLC
Chambersburg PA
CBHW072151160426
43197CB00012B/2338